Men! Fight for Me

Men! Fight for Me

■ ■ ■

*The Role of Authentic Masculinity
in Ending Sexual Exploitation
and Trafficking*

Alan Smyth • Jessica Midkiff

Printed in the United States of America

First Printing, 2021

ISBN-13: 978-1-954968-38-7 print edition
ISBN-13: 978-1-954968-39-4 ebook edition

DreamSculpt Books and Media
An imprint of:

Waterside Productions

Waterside Productions
2055 Oxford Ave
Cardiff, CA 92007
www.waterside.com

*This book is dedicated to the thousands of children
yet to be recovered and restored
from the horrific abuse of sex trafficking.*

*May you, the reader, find unrest and
be moved into action.*

The pimp who kidnapped me branded me like I was his slave. He was now my owner, and I saw no way out. I was considered to be a piece of his property, and I was treated as subhuman. I lived each and every day in survival mode, not sure if I was going to live or die. With my new life I received a new name, or so I thought. I was called "bitch" so often that it became my identity. I typically had over ten sexual encounters every single day. I felt as if, at any moment, anybody could have killed me. I began to prepare for my death.

Jessica Midkiff

For the first five months, I was fighting and trying to figure out how I could escape. But then, as I began to believe how worthless I had become, I could no longer fight for myself, and I gave up. <u>I needed someone to fight for me!</u>

Rachel Thomas

Foreword

The ultimate measure of a man is not where he stands in moments of comfort and convenience, but where he stands at times of challenge and controversy.

Martin Luther King, Jr

When we see things that are wrong in the world, we should work to make them right. Our culture and history esteem justice, and "justice" is the practice of making wrong things right. In the world today, I see something that is very wrong. I see an explosion of exploitation that human traffickers are unleashing on millions of men, women, boys, and girls. These traffickers strip away victims' personal liberty and attempt to deny their human dignity as they commit their crime. Whether through forced labor or sex trafficking, traffickers are treating inherently valuable people as a disposable commodity. Something must be done. We must bring justice by righting this wrong.

I never set out to combat human trafficking, but I found the issue compelling, the work meaningful, and the stories of freedom inspiring. I began working forced labor and sex trafficking cases in rural India before turning my attention to trafficking cases in the United States. For over a decade, I served as a federal prosecutor in the US Department of Justice's Human Trafficking Prosecution Unit. I also co-founded the Human Trafficking Institute and then had the honor of serving as the United States Ambassador-at-Large to Monitor and Combat Trafficking in Persons. So I've had "boots on the ground" and have been fighting to preserve human dignity for everyone for most of my career. I have been fortunate to spent time with survivors, investigators, trauma counselors, policy makers, educators, and people in organizations trying to figure out how we can stop traffickers, care for survivors, and work to prevent this crime.

Saving Innocence is one such anti-trafficking organization, located in Los Angeles. Their mission is to recover, restore, and bring justice to child victims of sex trafficking. I have been impressed with Saving Innocence's model and innovative strategy to deal with this important subset of human trafficking cases. I had the privilege of meeting co-author Alan Smyth through his work there. So when he asked me to write the foreword to this book, I knew it was because we share a common goal—to serve and to see the end of sex trafficking.

Alan co-authored this book with Jessica Midkiff, who survived ten years of sex trafficking and has spent an additional ten years as an advocate helping younger victims back to health and wholeness. As you read this book, you'll hear her story along with a variety of different perspectives on this issue. In chilling detail, you'll hear other survivors tell their harrowing stories of being trafficked, how their traffickers coerced them, and how they ultimately found freedom. You'll hear from a former trafficker, you'll get insights from law enforcement and men who have served on human trafficking task forces, and you'll get viewpoints on the topic of authentic masculinity from a variety of men from different walks of life. Ultimately, you'll have the opportunity to step up to the plate and get involved. This book ends with practical actions for you to consider that will help combat sex trafficking. As you can tell from the title, this book is directed at men. The book's focus doesn't imply that women have no role to play in this work. Instead, the focus on men highlights that there is something unique and important for men in this arena. In the context of sex trafficking, the vast majority of sex buyers are men, and the majority of traffickers are men. A distorted and toxic view of masculinity has done real damage in our culture. The authors are calling us to an authentic view of what it means to live well as a man, to live generously, and to live in a way that acknowledges the deep value all people (including women) possess. The authors are sending a clear message and strong challenge to all men—to step up to the plate, to own your role in this matter, and to take the steps that are necessary to make wrong things right. The lack of authentic, healthy, and positive masculinity has reached a crisis point in our country. If enough men to rise up, lead, and serve, it would make a tremendous difference.

The title of this book was inspired by an actual sex trafficking victim, and one of the things she said served as a clarion cry for Alan, and I hope it will for you as well. "I needed someone to fight for me." To be clear, this isn't a cartoonish call for men to ride in heroically and save the helpless damsel in distress. It isn't machismo or paternalism. The authors make clear that men have a constructive, authentic, and collaborative role to play in this fight.

I hope after reading the victims' stories and hearing from the people daily immersed in this work, that you will rise to the occasion, challenge yourself to develop your own version of authentic masculinity, and fight to right the wrongs that are happening right this minute on the streets of cities across this country and around the world.

Human trafficking is a worldwide criminal enterprise that people of goodwill must confront, disrupt, and stop. Justice demands that traffickers not commodify and dehumanize inherently valuable people. Valuing human dignity requires all of us to act, and reading this book is an excellent first step. The hope of freedom and human flourishing animates this work and inspires us to continue the fight.

John Cotton Richmond
Former United States Ambassador-at-Large to Monitor
and Combat Trafficking in Persons
Co-founder of the Human Trafficking Institute

Table of Contents

Introduction   xv

Part 1: Setting the Stage   1
Chapter 1 It's Our Job   3
Chapter 2 Owned—The Life: Jessica's Story   11
Chapter 3 Fight For Me: Rachel's Story   19
Chapter 4 Man-To-Man   31

Part 2: The Big Three   43
Chapter 5 The Buyers   47
Chapter 6 The Traffickers   65
Chapter 7 The Victims   81

Part 3: Conclusions and Solutions   99
Chapter 8 Looking in the Mirror   101
Chapter 9 Profiles in Authentic Masculinity   125
Chapter 10 Your 9/11 Moment   147
Epilogue: More Than a Survivor   153

Appendices Table of Contents   175
Appendix A: How to Report Human Trafficking   177
Appendix B: Contact Information   179
Appendix C: Warning Signs of Human Trafficking   181

Appendix D: Things You Can Do Today!   183
Appendix E: Things Your Church Can Do   185
Appendix F: Resources for Pornography Addiction   193
Appendix G: "More Than a Survivor" Bios   195
Appendix H: Recommended Resources   204
   Prevention—*The Cool Aunt* Series   204
   Sex + Money Documentary   205
   Recommended Books   206
Appendix I: CSEC   207
Appendix J: The Man in the Arena   210

Contributors   211
Acknowledgments   213
Notes   217
About the Authors   221

"Our lives begin to end the day we become silent about things that matter."

Martin Luther King, Jr.

Introduction

Years ago, in one of the great sports rants of all time, the Oklahoma State football coach declared, "I'm a man. I'm 40." If you are a college football fan, you know exactly what I'm talking about. In fact, you probably finished the sentence for me. If this phrase doesn't ring a bell, do yourself a favor and look up "Mike Gundy rant" and relive the magic as this football coach defends one of his players. I love this rant on so many levels.

I am also a man, and I'm… well… a bit over 40. I remember being 40. Does that count? I've been a man my entire life, over half a century. I guess that makes me an expert on the subject of men. I like sports, action movies, pizza, diet coke, and margaritas. I go to the gym most mornings, and I listen to Bon Jovi while enjoying the sauna after a workout. I like to get my mind right for the day by listening to "It's my life, it's now or never, but I ain't gonna live forever." That gets me fired up for action and ready to attack the day ahead of me!

I am a husband to an amazing wife of 36 years and a father to two great kids and one fantastic daughter-in-law. I'm one of the lucky dads who got to experience parenting from both sides. I loved both experiences of parenting a little girl as well as a little boy. I coached all their youth league teams, even soccer, which I knew nothing about. I attended most field trips, and I walked with them through adolescence and into adulthood. I even had the honor of performing the marriage ceremony of my son to his outstanding wife, Katy. I take pride in the fact that our house became the "go-to" place for my kids and their friends as they were growing up. A steady supply of my wife's "practically famous" cookies was definitely part of the attraction. However, I'd like to think that my kids and their friends felt welcomed and loved. Plus, we made sure to have plenty of fun things to do at our house, which didn't hurt.

My wife handled the heavy academics while I coached the teams and helped with projects. My claim to fame was the fourth-grade mission video for which we've had years of laughter revisiting the outtakes. One time, I helped my daughter construct a maze where we tested a live mouse's ability to remember how to find some food. Sadly, the lesson we learned that day had more to do with the food chain and survival of the fittest than it did with rodent memory. The guest instructor for our real-life lesson was our cat, Sweetie. It has been the joy of my life to be the dad of these two kids.

I'm a big movie guy. *Braveheart* stands alone at the top, and the second-place movie isn't even close. Best movie franchise is *Rocky*, of course. And if you can "handle the truth," one of the greatest dramas is *A Few Good Men*. I've never been a huge sci-fi guy, but *The Matrix* trilogy was certainly groundbreaking. The special effects were ridiculous, and I particularly liked that scene in the first installment when Neo had an important choice to make.

(Caution: gratuitous movie reference ahead.)

Neo was confronted with the option to either take the red pill or the blue pill. The red pill basically caused him to wake up. It allowed him to see reality and what the world had truly become. The blue pill caused him to stay asleep and go on living in his false reality, oblivious to real life and the real struggles that real people faced. You are now faced with a similar choice.

By reading this book, you will be taking the red pill. You will, in a sense, be awakened to the brutal realities of this world. If you would rather go on not knowing and remain oblivious, I suggest you take the blue bill and put this book down right now. The deal with Neo and the red pill is the same with us today. Once you take the red pill, there is no going back. You can't unsee what you will see, and you can't unknow what you will learn. If you continue, I thank you for having the courage of Neo and for being willing to take the red pill.

I have been encouraged by an internal voice as well as a few external voices to write this book. I suppose I have a unique perspective to add to an important conversation. I have spent my entire adult life working with kids. After 35 years with Young Life, it was time for me to leave. However, my heart was not yet finished with kids who are hurting. Not by a long shot.

I began to learn about this ridiculous reality in our country called human trafficking. Specifically, child sex trafficking. Even if you are not sure what that all entails, just the sound of it should conjure up horrible thoughts and images. "Child sex trafficking?" My first thought was that I had heard of things like this in other parts of the world. I was horrified to learn that it was running rampant right here in our country, in our cities, in every zip code, and with our own American-born kids.

I regularly attend various trainings, meetings, and other events related to the topic of human trafficking. When I show up, something incredibly obvious happens. It takes me about two seconds to understand that there are very few, if any, other men present. There are lots of brave, strong, passionate women involved at every level of this solution. However, the biggest part of this problem is caused by MEN. So where are all the men who should be trying to fix it? We have caused deep and significant pain in this world, and it's on us to step up and take leadership in the remedy.

Why is my voice important to this work? Because this problem is mostly caused by men. While both genders are definitely involved as perpetrators and victims, men are the primary sellers, and it is men who are the primary buyers. Something has gone horribly wrong with men. Of course, not all men have gone down this dark path, but the dark path is definitely filled with men. I believe that I have some of the antidote, and I feel a responsibility to speak to men. Man-to-man.

In this book, I will include lots of man-to-man real talk. My goal is to help as many men as possible gain a basic understanding of the modern-day slavery that is robbing us of our innocence. The first task is to make everyone aware! How in the world can we fix something that we don't even know exists? There is no right-thinking person who thinks the exploitation and purchase of kids for sex is acceptable. Of course not! Job One is to make sure everybody knows about it. And in this case, my target audience is specifically men. There are lots of women already passionately involved, so the gaping hole in the solution is the lack of strong men willing to take a stand and say, "Not on my watch." This is my niche. Although I certainly invite all the ladies to read this book and get further involved, I will be attempting to communicate directly to the male audience from my male perspective.

I'll spend a little time describing the dark and ugly crime being committed, mostly through real-life accounts of survivors who were courageously willing to share their story. In Chapter 2, I'll introduce you to my co-author, and you'll hear her firsthand account of her shocking experiences in "the life." You'll hear the heartbreaking reality she lived and survived. This part of the book will not be easy to read, but it's important that I grab your attention right from the beginning and show you the horrors of what's happening with our children. You will likely have a myriad of emotions ranging from shock, disgust, anger, and frustration to disbelief and confusion. And that's okay. I challenge you to sit in those emotions and let them keep you up at night. Let them simmer. Somewhere in the darkness, you will be inspired to act.

In Chapter 3, you'll hear the bone-chilling account of a college girl who was trafficked for sex. She could have easily been anyone's daughter. You'll learn that the title of this book comes directly from her words when she said, "I needed someone to fight for me."

However, rest assured we won't stay in the dark places too long. It can be overwhelming and simply too much to handle if you stay there forever. I work at a place where statements like these are part of the regular conversation. "Raped at knifepoint," "kidnapped," "pregnant at 14," "shot five times," "held hostage in a motel room," and "she is seven years old." It can be a lot when you realize the context of those statements is that they are happening to children in our midst. Our kids in our communities. We will also include stories and firsthand accounts of hope and accomplishments. You'll meet a few of my heroes along the way.

I have been deeply involved in the work of anti-human trafficking for five years. I give honor, thanks, and respect to all those who have been laboring in this field far longer than I. I don't consider myself an expert, but rather a dad who has been given a unique view into the crime of child trafficking. I am also someone who has never been afraid to use my voice when necessary. As a parent and a husband, the reality of sex trafficking is shocking, heartbreaking, and enraging. One friend recently called it "soul-crushing." I have walked with the survivors as well as the heroes who wade into this pain every single day. I have cried more in the past few years than in my previous 35 years of working with kids. I am fueled by a strong sense of justice and the ever-present thought of, *What if one of my own children were captured into this?*

This book will offer a road map to abolishment with a strong challenge to every man, including a little parenting advice along the way. As you work your way through this book gaining important knowledge and insight, rest assured that an unmistakable call to action will be coming at the end. There will be plenty of practical takeaways and action items for anyone who is ready to act. I'm excited for you to join me in this life-changing journey. You are reading this book for such a time as this!

I humbly submit this book to be used as a tool to help accomplish hope and healing where it's needed the most. There is a choice to be made. Child rape is being allowed to happen in our country. We can continue to allow this to happen, or we can decide to end it. There is something you can do! And you can start today. Brace yourselves and come with me on this journey. The estimated 300,000 children being trafficked for sex in our country need you to engage. They need strong MEN who will fight for them!

Come with me on this journey, and together we can create much-needed change!

Part 1
Setting the Stage

"We are not to simply bandage the wounds of victims beneath the wheels of injustice, we are to drive a spoke into the wheel itself."

Dietrich Bonhoeffer

1

It's Our Job

My Saving Innocence Journey Begins Here

I found myself in the middle of a career change after 25 years of going in the same direction. I had not considered it before, but it was now time for a change. For the first time in my adult life, I was seriously considering what was next. I was at a crossroads, wondering if I should stay with the organization that I had loved and given my life to for 35 years (25 on staff, ten as a volunteer), perhaps in an international role? I could have easily done that. It would have been the safe and comfortable thing to do. That would have been easy. However, my heart wouldn't release me from investing in the lives of troubled kids in Los Angeles. As days became months, I was committed to remaining open to all options. I was determined not to say yes or no to anything too quickly. I had a number of conversations for potential landing spots; however, none of them resonated with who I was and what I truly cared about.

My scope of consideration had several obvious components. I have a long history in building a nonprofit organization. I have years of experience in public speaking and leading teams. I've also done a considerable amount of fundraising along the way. Additionally, I have a strong passion for encouraging and helping to equip dads who are raising daughters. I was honored to collaborate on my first book entitled *Prized Possession*, which speaks to the vital importance of a relationship between dads and their daughters. I have enjoyed the privilege of leading many seminars for dads in an effort to help them understand how to effectively engage with their daughters in a more intentional way.

I'm a fighter by nature, although more figuratively than literally. As I previously mentioned, my all-time favorite movie is *Braveheart*. The highlight of that movie is William Wallace's impassioned battlefield speech to his troops, calling for "FREEDOM!" I have a strong passion to fight for those who cannot fight for themselves. I feel compelled to provide a voice for those who have been silenced and cannot speak for themselves. *There must be some place*, I thought, *where my passion combined with my life experience could help bring freedom to the oppressed. And a place where the "silenced" might be heard through my voice.*

I had become aware of a stellar nonprofit organization based in Los Angeles called Saving Innocence. I was aware that they were involved with child victims of sex trafficking. However, I had only a very broad, 30,000-foot view of their work. Still, that bullet point alone was enough to capture my attention and fuel my next step. Child victims of sex trafficking? What other group of people is in greater need of a strong voice fighting passionately on their behalf? After a cold call to set up a meeting, my car and my heart drove straight to the front door of Saving Innocence.

I had contacted the organization's founder, Kim Biddle, via text. After making a virtual self-introduction, I texted, "I'd love to meet with you to hear more of your story." Fortunately, she accepted my invitation. We met, and after a brief tour of their office, we sat down for a conversation that would change the trajectory of my life. I informed her that 50 percent of this meeting was me being really interested in this topic and wanting to know more as a dad with a daughter and as someone who has given his life to the enrichment of kids' lives. The other 50 percent was me exploring options for a career change. I let her know that I had no idea if they were hiring. I had no idea if there was even an appropriate place for a man to be involved in an organization such as this. I didn't know what I didn't know. However, the one thing I was certain of was that my heart was unmistakably pulling me in this direction.

Kim went on to share with me some of her personal story that eventually led to her founding Saving Innocence. She further educated me on the shocking scope of this problem—that there are thousands of children being trafficked in Southern California alone, and some estimate as many as 300,000 nationwide. Most of these aren't kids being shipped in from other countries. They are American-born US citizens who are right here within our own communities. She added, to my astonishment, that this is happening in all 50 states without regard for socioeconomic boundaries. No community was immune. I was mesmerized and perplexed. My thoughts were going in a thousand different directions—the least of which was the thought that this meeting was going long and I would surely have a $68 parking ticket waiting on my windshield. But it would be a small price to pay for such an impactful and eye-opening education!

Kim described the unique role that Saving Innocence plays in this solution. I learned about her team of rock star case managers who are on call 24/7. I learned that when law enforcement officials recover one of these children, the call goes out to Saving Innocence and one of their heroes responds to the scene anywhere in LA County within 90 minutes.

Suddenly, everything I held dear and all of my previous relationships and experiences began to make sense. I had an overwhelming feeling that the sum total of all that I had done and endeavored to do in my previous life experiences and relationships had culminated in this purpose—right here and right now. As the meeting ended, my thought process was just getting started because I knew I had to be a part of this in some way. I told Kim as much prior to leaving the building. I told her that I would at least become a small donor, although I hoped for more than that.

I left that day with two thoughts:
1. How is this happening?
2. I have to do something. I'm IN … whatever that means. Joining this fight resonates with who I am at the deepest core of my being and in every fiber of my DNA.

In the days and weeks that followed, my mind was fixated on these children who have become captives at the hands of evil personified. Just to clarify, when I say "children," I've learned that the average age of entry is just 12 years old. That's the **average** age!

I suddenly began to notice things I hadn't noticed before. My eyes were now opened to a new paradigm that I previously didn't even realize existed. I had taken the "red pill" and was now awakened to a new reality—the actual reality—and there was no going back.

My wife and I were fortunate enough to stay at a friend's beach house soon after my meeting with Kim. I had been reading articles and watching videos on the topic. My mind was being inundated and my heart had been pulverized. While sleeping one night at this beach house, I was awakened by a vivid dream. In my dream, I saw myself going into one of these brothels that I had been learning about. I approached what appeared to be a 13-year-old girl. I knew why she was there. I took her by the elbow and said, "C'mon, I'm getting you out of here." We walked out the front door and got into my car. I sped off while looking in the rearview mirror to see if anyone was chasing me. It was at that point that I woke up and was unable to fall back asleep. It might sound more like a movie scene, but I took that dream as something of a sign. Perhaps in this next chapter of my life, I was supposed to not only use my voice but give myself to the liberation of children.

My meeting with Kim had now advanced to a conversation with the board chair to further consider what my role might be. After another thorough discussion, I communicated the obvious. "I have a lot to learn about human trafficking. However, I know a lot of people who have no idea you even exist, and they have no idea this problem exists. My job description for the last twenty-five years has been to recruit, train, plan, fundraise, present, and build a nonprofit organization. And for the last fourteen years, I have been doing that in Los Angeles." I made one more thing clear as we continued to process my possible future at Saving Innocence. "Listen, I know things are tight financially for you right now. I want to make one thing clear. There is no way I will get paid anything that I don't first bring in. I have a network of supporters who are just waiting for me to let them know what I'm doing next." I felt like it was kind of a no-brainer of sorts. I was offering to come and work for them to help further the mission, and I was guaranteeing them that it wouldn't cost them a dime.

After a formal board interview, I was extended an offer to join the team, which I quickly accepted. It is my honor to partner with these great people—these heroes—at Saving Innocence who are working tirelessly, every day, to bring health and wholeness to these extremely traumatized young victims. What a surreal turn of events. I had accepted a job in a field that I did not even know existed just a few months earlier. The learning curve would certainly be steep.

My ongoing exposure to this important work has further opened my eyes and given me a unique platform from which to speak and help end this horrendous abuse perpetrated on young children in the name of profit. This book is coming from real life experiences, and I am pleased to enlighten you to what I have discovered.

My goal with this book is to issue a strong challenge to men everywhere. My hope is that men will live differently and seek to bring healing to this broken world. We need men to become liberators at a time when many have become weak and passive, at best, and oppressors, at worst!

My hope and prayer is that millions of men will lean into this tragic issue and make a decision to end human trafficking. **Spoiler Alert:** Actually, my goal is much higher than that. My hope and prayer is that men will rise up and be the kind of men they were intended to be. The lack of authentic, healthy, and positive masculinity has reached a crisis point in our country. If we can get enough men to rise up, lead, and serve as they were meant to, one of the many results of those actions will be the end of human trafficking. However, in the process, we'll cure a myriad of other ills as well. I will use human trafficking as the worst possible example of how men have gone wrong in hopes of bringing all men into the bigger conversation of living out their God-given calling and stepping into the kind of man who creates healing rather than pain.

It's not someone else's job. It's our job.

**"It wasn't my fault.
I had no choice. It was survival."**

Survivor, age 16

2

Owned—The Life: Jessica's Story

The activity surrounding an individual who is being actively trafficked is called "the life," or "the game." This includes the grooming or luring in by a predator, followed by the active buying and selling of the victim. One of the highlights of my time at Saving Innocence has been meeting and getting to know some of these amazingly resilient survivors. What they have gone through is mind-boggling. I am in awe of what they have been forced to endure and the aftermath of what they still must carry. Being bought, sold, and abused by more men than they can count, seven days a week, is beyond comprehension. I have been exposed to a very dark world and have seen, first-hand, the effects of what this abusive life has done to young girls and women. However, before we delve any deeper and even consider possible solutions, I would like to share with you a personal account from one of my colleagues who is all too familiar with this life.

Meet my colleague and co-author, Jessica, whom I am honored to call my friend. She is also my hero, by the way. There are few who are as strong and as uniquely resilient as she is. She has conquered so much from enduring over ten years of oppressive abuse and traumatic exploitation. Her personal knowledge and accomplishment in escaping it is beyond significant and second to none. As my co-author, she will not only share her personal story in this chapter, but she will also contribute significantly from her wealth of insight and personal experiences throughout the rest of this book. You can trust what she says on this topic because she has firsthand accounts and so much lived experience.

Jessica is a brave, smart, faithful leader in the movement to end sex trafficking. I urge you to read her words slowly, carefully, repeatedly, and respectfully. Let them sink in. Let them bother you, and may they move you one step closer to unmistakable action.

CAUTION: The following content will not be easy to digest. It won't be easy to read, and it won't be easy to forget. Proceed with caution as I proudly introduce you to a living hero.

Jessica's Story

I look at the tattoo on my neck as a battle scare. It's a cover-up. There used to be a name under it. The pimp who kidnapped me branded me like I was his slave, and it was done against my will. I received this tattoo when I wasn't sure if I was going to get killed that night or not. I felt new levels of fear as I went completely numb during this process.

This demeaning symbol of ownership made it clear to me that my life was no longer my own. I had a profound feeling of being stuck and I was unable to move. One thing I was sure of the night I received it was that I didn't want to die, and I would do whatever I had to do in order to live. This was my life, and I was now living it one moment at a time.

A lot of our young girls today have brandings on their face or their neck. They are usually branded a few places all over their bodies. The girls I work with see my tattoos and automatically identify with me. They can trust me because they know that I understand what they are going through.

My story of abuse began at a very young age. My mother was a teen mom and had me when she was 17. My father left when I was a baby. From the very beginning, I had a feeling of not being wanted and the feeling of being inadequate. I grew up with a constant and profound sense of rejection. That lead me down the path of searching for approval and acceptance from men, no matter who they were or what they did.

My grandmother took care of me for the first few years of my life. My mom left on what you might say was a "personal journey" to find herself. She came back for me when I was three years old. By then, she had already married another man, and that's when the real abuse began. It started out with him sexually abusing me; then it turned into him trying to kill me. Among other things, he held my head underwater in the bathtub, pushed me down a flight of stairs, and put me in an oven. As a young girl, I was made to believe that I had always done something wrong and that I was "bad" and needed to be punished. He beat me on a regular basis, and I watched my mom being beaten as well. The sexual abuse started at the age of three, and it continued to happen until the age of six. My mother and I were both being abused at the same time. By the time I was nine years old, there were men coming in and out of my house who were trying to sleep with me and trying to get different sexual favors from me.

By the time I was 11, all this trauma and abuse had sent me down a path of low self-esteem and the need for survival.

Food was scarce and so were many other basic necessities. There were guys coming to the house who were willing to provide for my various wants and needs in exchange for sexual favors. At age 11, I started to clean houses. Men were paying the "cleaning fee" while they abused me sexually in their homes. I particularly remember a nasty 50-year-old man who raped me at one of these house cleaning appointments. He portrayed himself as a nice man with good intentions masquerading as a father figure to lower my guard. However, nothing could have been farther from the truth. This happened repeatedly for years. When I was 14, I was jumped into one of the local LA gangs. My life in the gang community didn't last long, however, because I never really had a gang mentality. At 14, I hated my life and most definitely was not a happy kid.

Soon, a young gang member built a rapport and developed a relationship with me (I didn't know he was only 15 at the time). He was learning "the game" and was always suggesting sex for money. The traditional "trafficking" part of my story started the day I got into a bad fight with my mom. I ran away from her and fell right into the young exploiter's business plan.

He began to exploit me at 14 years of age, and not surprisingly, I was his first victim. In my mind, I was escaping all the abuse I had already gone through. My family and their friends were constantly abusing me and threatening to kill me. I decided I would rather be abused by strangers than be abused by people close to me. I can't tell you how many times I've been raped out on the streets, and it doesn't hurt as much as the abuse I received from my own family.

When I was 15, I was able to get out of the life for a brief period of time. I was pregnant with my daughter, and I moved into a group home. I was lured back into the life in order to pay the mounting bills. Since I was never formally in the child welfare system, I was forced to pay my own bills. I was taught to lie to social workers in order to keep my family together. Soon, I had multiple pimps over the course of several years who were trafficking me across state lines. During that time, I was trafficked in Arizona, Nevada, Texas, Florida, and Washington, DC. I was even trafficked across the street from the White House on occasion. Not quite the way most people envision seeing our country.

When I was 17 years old, I had two long ponytails. One night I was followed by some men on Figueroa Street, a common "track" in Los Angeles. They said I was cute and that I looked like Pocahontas. They had a gun, and I was afraid. They told me not to scream or they would "beat the hell out of me and then kill me." There were approximately 30 men there that night, and I was raped all night long. That's the night I got branded on my neck. After I was branded, you can't imagine what the next few years were like. I was hog-tied, put in trunks of cars, and pistol-whipped. I jumped and rolled out of cars. I was beaten up and raped repeatedly. I was called "bitch" every single day, over and over, so much so that I would forget what my real name was. It became normal. Typically, I had over ten sexual encounters every day. It was one thing after another, and that's when the trauma fully set in for me. I felt as if, at any moment, anybody could have killed me. I began to prepare for my death.

The things I saw were beyond disturbing. At times, the pimps even had girls in dog cages. In one of the houses I was in, there were at least 12 cages. Girls were being water-boarded as punishment, and they were being sold over and

15

over. They were trying to break these girls and having other guys coming in, having sex with them and getting paid. I lived every girl's worst nightmare, and I saw so many others in the same boat. This season of my trafficking experience went on for three straight years with no break. I was exhausted.

I was able to get out of the life when I was 20 years old. It had been a long, painful stretch of abuse. After so much trauma over the years, I had reached a point of total exhaustion. At some point, I had resigned myself to what had become normal and acceptable. I began to believe the lies that this is what I was meant to do and I could never be anything more. So many of the girls being trafficked need to be emotionally ready to leave before they are actually able to leave. Even though things were rough the entire time, at this point, I was finally ready to exit this torturous existence. Looking back, I feel as if God was pushing me out of the life and making a way of escape. I crossed paths with a shop owner who came into my life at just the right moment. He provided me with some basic necessities, and I was finally on my way out! It's not easy to get out of the life for many reasons, and there were plenty of bumps in the road. It's never easy to change your lifestyle, especially when it's built on a lifetime of lies, abuse, and deception.

It's not safe on the street for anyone, and especially for children. Since my exit from the life, I have worked with girls as young as 11 years old. Looking into their eyes, I saw myself in their story, and I desperately wanted to help them avoid the road that I traveled. It's so hard to see the patterns of abuse continuing in the next generation of kids.

While those years of my life were incredibly abusive and traumatizing, I consider myself fortunate to have escaped when I did. I could have easily wound up as just another statistic like so many others have. Sometimes I think of what could have become of me had I not gathered enough strength to make my way out. I have friends who never made it out. Like a good friend of mine who was burned alive and left in a garbage can. I'm so grateful to have my life as it is today and to be able to raise my amazing daughter. I am extremely thankful for those who helped me escape and recover from my exploitation. There is so much more to my life, and my story is not done being written.

Thank you for learning about my life and the life that so many others are still living. What you just read is a pretty common description of what many thousands of kids in our country are going through right now. I shared the story of my personal journey with you because I want you to have a better understanding of what is actually going on out there every single day and what so many kids are currently dealing with. I want you to know some of the factors that create the vulnerabilities that lead to the exploitation of children. I don't share my experiences lightly or easily. I do so because I trust that my story will help motivate you into action. I trust that part of my redemption story will include you being motivated to end the exploitation of women and children.

Tonight, when you tuck your kids into bed, you can imagine the hundreds of thousands of kids just getting ready to go out to "work." My hope and prayer would be for you to be impacted enough to ask more questions and ultimately get involved in this fight. My only request of you is that you respect me for sharing all of this personal information enough to take some kind of action. Children and young women like me need you to fight for them.

"Victory is always possible for the person who refused to stop fighting."

Napoleon Hill

3

Fight for Me: Rachel's Story

I attended a gathering that further confirmed the trajectory I was on in the fight against human trafficking, specifically child sex trafficking. Two members of the Saving Innocence staff, Jessica and Kim Biddle, were invited to participate in a panel discussion at an awareness event. I was there to offer support to my team and to connect with anyone in the room in need of additional information. Little did I know that I would be the one on the receiving end of some very insightful information and deeply motivating inspiration that would rock my world!

Included on the panel of six was a woman named Rachel Thomas. She is the founder of an important organization called Sowers Education Group. Their mission is "Sowing seeds of human trafficking awareness and survivor empowerment." I invite you to visit their website to learn more at www.sowerseducationgroup.com. Additionally, she created *The Cool Aunt* series, which is a phenomenal video series providing education for teens regarding the warning signs, risk factors, and tactics of traffickers. Every teen should watch this series!

Rachel shared her personal story that day, as she has done many times before. At the conclusion of her story, she ended with a jarring statement that caused the hair on the back of my neck to stand up. I asked Rachel if I could share her story here, and she gave me her permission. The following is some of what she shared that day. It concludes with the very powerful statement that inspires and motivates me to continue my personal commitment to helping liberate as many children as I can! I sincerely hope it will inspire you as well.

Hopes and Dreams

I came from a great family environment in suburban Los Angeles. My parents were well-educated, and I grew up in a very stable, happy upper-middle-class home. I had a lot going for me. I played volleyball, ran track, and was a prom queen with a 3.8 grade point average. In the household that I came from, it was expected and assumed that I'd go to college. It's what you do. You graduate high school and then you go to college, just like both of my parents and my older sister did. So after I graduated high school, I went to college at Emory University in Atlanta, Georgia. Like everyone who goes to college, I had hopes and dreams of getting an education along with some fun and adventure. One of the things I had always dreamed of was being a teacher. I used to line up my dolls and teach them lessons on various topics with my little chalkboard and little pieces of chalk, so I anticipated that college would help me realize my lifelong dream of becoming a teacher.

I majored in English because I love reading books and writing and thought that teaching English would be the perfect fit for me.

I didn't really have any fears about going to college. Like most savvy young women today, I was armed with the basic safety precautions such as don't walk alone at night and don't

let anyone slip something into your drink. I was naïve enough
to think that was all I needed to know.

I loved school and thrived during my first two years. I lived
in the dorm, was a regular on the dean's list, and had lots of
friends. I would describe myself in those years as someone
who liked to party and have fun but also was a nerd. My biggest worry at that time was not getting good grades.

Junior Year

It was in my junior year that I met "Mike." He was a polite, well-
spoken, professional-looking man in a three-piece suit. He told
me that he was a modeling agent and that I had great potential to be a model. While handing me a business card, he told
me he knew talent when he saw it, and that I had what it took.
He offered to invest in my modeling career and assured me
that he could secure me a paid modeling job within a month.
I was a little hesitant to accept his card, but he seemed very
polite and passionate about my potential, so I decided to call
him the next day to talk further. I ended up taking him up on his
offer to invest in my modeling career.

The first photo was his initial investment, and the shoot
had the look and feel of a legit operation. There were professional lights, cameras, photographers, makeup artists, ward-
robe racks, other models and everything else that a teen would
consider to be a professional, top-notch shoot. After that, he
started talking about photo shoots and major auditions in New
York City. My soon-to-be trafficker was pushy, but in a polite
and flattering way. When his plans for me conflicted with my
school or extracurricular activities, he didn't like to take no for
an answer. He would say things like, "You are in the prime of
your life and you look better than ninety-nine percent of the

population. You should use the gifts that God has given you."
He was a master at manipulation via flattery. He made me
believe that he was really excited to work with me.

After getting booked for my first paid modeling job, Mike
asked me to fill out a W9, which included my parents' home
address and my social security number. About a month into
our model and agent relationship, in what had seemed like
a normal process, I officially signed on with his modeling
agency. He told me his fee would be $25,000, which sounded
like a lot, but I figured I could pay that off in just a few months
with the modeling jobs he had already found for me. It was
almost immediately after I signed the contract that I was
informed of the expectations of my new "job." I was ordered
to respond to appointments he made for me and to have sex
with various customers. I immediately pushed back, but my
new boss told me: "Bitch, I own you now, and you're going
to do what I tell you to do, or someone's gonna get hurt."
He then read aloud my parents' home address. I was both
horrified and terrified at the thought of what was happening
and what *could* happen if I didn't comply. I felt completely
deceived and trapped. I ended up being sold over and over
and forced to perform various sex acts with complete strangers. I had become the target of an insidious human trafficking scheme. Mike's "modeling agency" was actually a front
used to prey on bright, young college students away from
home and then exploit them under the threat of violence
and force.

I was a victim, but I wasn't on a street corner or on the
Internet. Mike would notice which men were buying dances
at the strip club I was forced to dance at and then he would
approach them and say, "You can have her for the night. I'll

bring her to you." It was despicable and degrading, but I felt like I had no way out.

Manipulation, Psychological Abuse—Trapped
It's natural to think, "Why didn't you run away or call the police!?" And trust me, I wanted to! But I was being physically abused and terrorized by real threats of harm to my parents. When I actually threatened to call the police on Mike, he said that he would kill me, my parents, and my roommate if I did. There were real threats on the lives of my parents and the people closest to me if I refused to comply with his demands.

The manipulation deepened with my trafficker when he pulled out the contract that I had signed stating that I owed him $25,000. He pointed to my signature and convinced me that I was legally bound to his service and that I owed him $25,000, one way or another. I felt completely hopeless and stuck. So, out of fear for my life, I resolved to work for him until I paid off my $25,000 debt. Once I had that paid off, I genuinely thought I would be free to leave. But I soon found out that wasn't the case, and he continued to sell me to other men under the threat and reality of violence and abuse. It was then that I realized that this was no longer about money, this was about ownership and control.

At this point, I really felt absolutely trapped. I felt like I had no one to turn to. Even members of the Atlanta police department were buyers. I was actually sold to uniformed police officers on more than one occasion, so in my mind, that eliminated the police as a viable option for help. The ruthless and violent nature of my trafficker kept me involved with him. After five months of being trafficked in this manner, I felt completely hopeless and helpless. I began to believe that I was a worthless piece of property with no hope of redemption and no possibility of escape. In essence, I had given up. It's difficult to fully grasp what a terrible predicament I was in. There's little wonder why thoughts of suicide began to creep in. I really believed that my only option for escape that wouldn't put my parents in danger was for me to kill myself. I made an attempt on my life by taking pills. I woke up with blood and vomit on my mouth when I had obviously failed. I didn't really want to kill myself, but I saw no other solutions to get out of this life.

So many of these traffickers gain control over their victims by isolating them, and that's what happened to me. I was emotionally isolated from the police, my parents, and my friends. I dropped out of my classes. The psychological abuse continued as he went on to manipulate me spiritually by saying that because I was a prostitute, I could no longer set foot in a church. This particular trafficker was quoting the Bible and twisting the scripture to further manipulate me into compliance. I was stripped of all resources and all hope. It was a time of being in a "very dark place" because when you're surrounded by such darkness and under its control, it's really hard to believe there is any goodness and light anywhere. Combined with the mounting guilt and shame, you begin to believe that this is where you belong. This is how your world operates.

For the first five months, I was fighting and trying to figure out a way to escape. However, after suffering the abuse and terror for months, I gave up and resigned myself to my new reality. I even continued to communicate with my parents two to three times a week, but I never told them what was happening to me. I told them that everything was great for fear of jeopardizing their safety if I were to ever let them know the truth. I was caught between the pain of my own abusive trauma and that of my parents' safety.

Call to Action

It was at this point in her story that Rachel uttered one of the most powerful statements I've ever heard. It had so much impact on me that it stopped me dead in my tracks and, at the same time, got me fired up for action! I found confirmation and resolution in her words when she said:

> "For the first five months, I was fighting and trying to figure out how I could escape. But then, as I began to believe how worthless I had become, I could no longer fight for myself, and I gave up. I needed someone to fight for me!"

I almost stood up in the crowded auditorium. Her statement confirmed what was already in my heart and the direction in which my life was now headed. I want to be someone fighting on behalf of those who can't fight for themselves, those who need someone to fight for them! When I think of the thousands of children who are victimized by this sex trafficking epidemic, I am forever motivated by the mere thought of kids out there wishing that someone would come and find them, fight for them, and help liberate them. Rachel informed me that victims might indeed want our help in the early stages of their exploitation, and many would likely be willing escapees. However, it is entirely possible that after a period of time, the severity of this life could very well have beaten them down into compliance and apathy. There may be thousands of kids out there right now who don't even know they need to be recovered and, in fact, might even resist our attempts. Their oppression and manipulation have convinced them of their hopelessness. On the other hand, there are children being abusively exploited and hoping that someone—anyone—will take the initiative to fight for them, provide a way out, and help them escape!

The reason that I almost stood up in that crowded auditorium is simply this: As I listened to Rachel's story, I couldn't help thinking that she looked a lot like my own daughter. They appeared to be of similar age. They were both high-achieving student-athletes from great homes where they were loved and encouraged by both parents. Each grew up knowing the protective love of their father, and they both went away to college. Rachel's story is riveting because she does not fit the typical profile of most sex trafficking victims, as you'll soon learn about in this book. Most sex trafficking victims are younger kids who have already experienced significant trauma in their life. Because of their age and their tumultuous early adolescence, they are experiencing a great deal of vulnerability. Rachel's story is important because I see the faces of average young girls like my own daughter's in her story.

Stop at Nothing

Indulge me for a moment. If my daughter were to be taken captive by a pimp and his deceptive and abusive tactics, I would stop at nothing to track her down, fight for her, and recover her at all costs. The movie TAKEN quickly comes to mind. Even though TAKEN is not thought to be incredibly authentic or accurate as far as how human trafficking usually works, I resonate deeply with the relentless pursuing heart of a father that is demonstrated in that movie. The main character, the father of the daughter who was abducted, stopped at nothing to rescue his daughter.

If I were to envision something similar happening to my family, upon hearing of what happened, there would be a hundred people on my front lawn asking what they could do. They would be passing out flyers and conducting social media campaigns to find her. There would be alerts on the freeway signs, and I would hire private detectives to work around the clock. To be clear, it would be World War III! I'm not sure I would ever sleep again until I found my daughter.

My point is this: My own daughter could have been Rachel. Your daughter could have been Rachel. Rachel's story confirms that the scourge of sex trafficking is not as far away as you might think!

So, why aren't there more people laboring in this field to recover these stolen young lives? Could it be that it has little to no personal impact on most of us? The disconnection of viewing this as someone else's problem breeds apathy toward public outrage or any large-scale effort to put an end to this horrific crime. If we don't take this crime personally, it won't be taken seriously. It has become commonplace to think that this is something that happens "somewhere over there," perhaps far away, to people that we do not know—and certainly not to anyone in our own family or community.

When Rachel said, "I needed someone to fight for me," it reverberated from my mind down into my heart. In that moment, I wished I could have been there to help her. I am wired to be that person for lost kids. I didn't recently develop this trait. It has always been there, but Rachel's words sharpened my focus and ignited my purpose!

Here is my challenge to anyone who will listen, and especially to the men reading this book. Let's respond, at least in part, as if these kids are someone we know and cared about. Dare I say we even view the victims as OUR OWN daughters or granddaughters? I can think of no worse reality for a child than to be bought and sold, over and over again, for the deviant sexual gratification of perverted adult men.

Additionally, to have their own lives threatened, and the lives of their families threatened if they refuse to comply, leaves them hopeless and without options. Let us *rise up* and engage in this battle. Engage as if it has hit home. Rachel reminds us that it actually could have. Sadly, it still might if we don't put an end to it, once and for all.

Let me remind you what the great Martin Luther King, Jr. once famously said:

"An injustice anywhere is a threat to justice everywhere."

There might be no greater injustice than the plague of sex trafficking forced upon children. Just because it hasn't happened to your own daughter does not excuse you from joining this fight. Men, we do not have a free pass on this. If we're going to win this fight, we're going to need you to get off the couch and engage in a meaningful way. I will spell out plenty of practical ways for you to get involved later in this book. For now, my goal is to paint a more complete picture of what is actually going on out there and what you can do about it. There are still some critical components to this puzzle we must talk about before you charge ahead and attempt to get involved.

First, we learn... then we act.

From the mouth of Rachel Thomas comes our call to action. "I needed someone to fight for me!"

WHO'S WITH ME???

"There is no passion to be found playing small,
In settling for a life that is less than the one you
are capable of living."

Nelson Mandela

"Somewhere inside, we hear a voice. It leads us
in the direction of who we wish to become. But it
is up to us whether or not to follow."

Pat Tillman

4

Man-To-Man

What does a conversation about true, powerful, positive, authentic masculinity have to do with sex trafficking? The answer is everything! The crime of sex trafficking is primarily perpetrated by unhealthy males. If we can get enough men to live out a better, truer, and more authentically positive version of themselves, then we can end the crime of human trafficking, not to mention a host of other problems along the way.

As you may have gathered by now, I'm a pretty big movie guy. To that end, I want to begin this important chapter by quoting two of my favorites.

The movie poster from my all-time greatest movie ever, *Braveheart*, quotes one of William Wallace's famous lines, which occurs late in the movie. At this point in the film, he is facing certain death for standing up for his principles and pushing back on extreme injustice. Just before he is ushered in to be executed, he says this:

"Every man dies, not every man really lives."

The message is clear, concise, and simple. You may be physically alive, but you may not be truly living. So, what does it mean to be truly *alive*? Too many men are going through the motions in life, just getting by from one day to the next. One compromise after another. Satisfying self. Stepping back instead of stepping forward. Seriously men, is that all there is? What are you fighting for? What are you living for? What are you ready to die for? I am looking for men who are in search of real life. True life. Authentic life and authentic masculinity. Only then can we dream of a better world free from injustice.

Another great movie, *Gladiator*, features Maximus fighting his way back from severe injustice against him, his deceased beloved leader, and his murdered family. I love his perspective on life and his focus on something bigger, something eternal. The *Gladiator* movie poster says this:

"What we do in life echoes in eternity."

Yes, I believe this is true. I believe what we do now impacts future generations. I also believe that we will all be held accountable for what we did or didn't do with the information we have been given. By the end of this book, you will have been given a wealth of information regarding child sex trafficking. What will you do with that information? Your answer may profoundly cause echoes in eternity!

It is literally *good versus evil*. We need an army of good, strong men to confront those evil men who have bad intentions. Weak, passive men stand as unwitting ushers, allowing access to a pathway for evil deeds to be done. And further, I would assert that these same men are found complicit in the wrong things they despise when they do nothing to confront them.

The great Dietrich Bonhoeffer, a German theologian who attempted to assassinate Adolf Hitler, clarifies things perfectly when he says the following: "Silence in the face of evil, is itself evil. God will not hold us guiltless. Not to speak is to speak. Not to act is to act."

Bonhoeffer puts us all on trial. He is essentially saying that our inaction is making a statement, and, in fact, it is helping the other side. Our silence is louder than you think. I agree with Bonhoeffer on this. If you remain silent in the face of wrongdoing, your apathy communicates that you agree with what is happening. We must go on record against the evil that is being perpetrated. You must ask yourself, Am I ready to be counted? Am I ready to stand up and say, no more? Am I ready to confront the abuse and injustice being perpetrated on young boys and girls in the name of pleasure and profit?

The dictionary defines "authentic" as "not false or copied; genuine; real."

The dictionary defines "masculinity" as "qualities or attributes regarded as characteristics of men."

To suggest that there is such a thing as "authentic masculinity," one must also assume that there is such a thing as *inauthentic* masculinity. I'm certain that we've all seen both versions played out, over and over. There is a warped and diminished version of what men are supposed to do and be as shaped by the media, culture, and a steady stream of fallacies. There is an important role that men should be playing in the lives of their families and their communities, yet it seems as though it has never been more difficult to do. There is little wonder why the world is in such a mess. Men are shrinking and channeling their strength toward the kingdom of *self*, and in the worst cases, they are directing their energy toward the destruction of others.

The world is full of counterfeits. We are constantly led to believe the wrong thing instead of what is right. What's worse is that promoting the wrong thing over and over eventually leads men to *believe* that it's actually the right thing. There is a healthy dose of lies being delivered right to our doorstep on a daily basis. Or should I say, delivered to the various media devices that we are tethered to on a regular basis. Our little girls are constantly lied to regarding their value, their worth, and the world's perception of beauty. Our little boys are consistently lied to regarding what their strength and purpose on this earth should be used for.

Tragically, our young boys are receiving constant and thorough training on "manhood" from unreliable sources, including hip-hop/rap/pop music, testosterone-laden video games, and even from their favorite sports heroes—not to mention the entertainment industry in general. Popular song lyrics from the most popular artists teach them that women are no more than property—a disposable "thing" to be sexually, even violently, used and discarded. This industry unashamedly promotes, normalizes, and glamorizes a rape culture for our boys to aspire to. Not to mention the constant objectification of women in advertising strategies. When there is a weak, passive father, or possibly no father figure at all, our little boys tend to follow the crowd. Unfortunately, it's often down a path that offers very few positive, healthy options or appropriate guidance. And to compound the dangers of the crowded path, it certainly offers no accountability for young boys' actions.

Without the consistent influence of a strong father or father figure providing the proper perspective on media and keeping a watchful eye on harmful messaging, there is a destructive storm on the horizon. We see this calamity manifest itself in numerous ways throughout society. The most extreme case is the subject matter being presented in this book. However, there are plenty of other destructive issues that flourish due to passivity in men and their failure to stand up and be strong.

My friend Brodie, a 25-year veteran of the United States Secret Service, told me something that really captured my attention. He shared with me that those members of law enforcement who are tasked with identifying and disrupting counterfeit currency rings have a profound way of doing their work. He said:

> "In order to spot the counterfeit currency, they spend nearly all of their time studying the real thing. With such intimate knowledge of the authentic version, it makes it easy to spot the counterfeit version a hundred miles away."

When it comes to masculinity, the lines have been blurred. On a regular basis, we are inundated with inauthentic counterfeit versions of masculinity that are harmfully toxic. We desperately need an infusion of the *real thing* into our culture.

So rather than spending a lot of time focusing on all of the horrible examples of how men are portrayed in the media or the ugly displays of character being portrayed daily in the entertainment industry, I would like to shift focus and shine a light on what the "real thing" looks like. To that end, I will share some personal thoughts on authentic masculinity in this chapter. I have also asked some friends to share some of their thoughts, and they will appear later in Chapter 9. My hope is that if we can take a moment and, collectively, focus on the *real thing,* it will be easier to spot the counterfeit and further provide a much-needed course correction.

I would like to offer some of my personal story. As I stated earlier, my wife and I raised a son, and I have done quite a bit of thinking about how to raise him to be a strong young man who's capable of making the world a better place. So, with humility, I would like to share some of what we did.

When my son, Trevor, was five years old, I came across a powerful book called *Raising a Modern-Day Knight,* by Robert Lewis. I highly recommend it for all dads who have sons. The author tackled this very topic of what it is to be a man and how a father can effectively transfer those traits to his son. He wanted to be certain that he was passing down all that his son needed to know in order to equip him to one day leave the nest and lead a healthy and productive life. I was taken with this book and immediately recruited my two good buddies Geoff and Ronnie, who had sons the same age as mine. I gave them each a copy of the book, and the three of us dads endeavored to proactively help our sons understand authentic masculinity starting at a young age. It was fun to cheer them on in their successes and be there for them in their challenges.

The first task we had was to put down on paper our definition of a man. It's a good question with no clear answer. Is a man defined by a certain age? His biology? His accomplishments? Does a boy become a man the first time he has sex? We thought about it for a while and had some great conversation around it. We needed to make it practical and tangible enough for our boys to grasp at a young age, yet meaningful enough for it to last a lifetime. We needed to give our sons the gift of clarity on this often confusing yet critical subject.

What is a man? When does a boy become one? And how can we raise real men who live out authentic masculinity? After much deliberation, we came up with our own four-pronged definition of a man that would shape the content of our father-son activities for years to come. Ultimately, our hope was to provide a lifelong road map for authentic masculinity. Plus, we had a blast doing this with our boys.

By the way, we called our father-son group "Braveheart." Because, why not? Strength, courage, fighting a battle bigger than ourselves, and confronting injustice against all odds—these are all the qualities we aimed to instill in our boys. The following is a four-pillar, working definition of a man that we established for our sons.

Pillar 1: He Accepts Responsibility
We need a generation of men to rise up and answer the call of responsibility in their lives. How often do we see men biologically become fathers yet are quick to abdicate their place of input and leadership in their children's lives? Too many women and children are suffering in this world because there are not enough real men taking responsibility for their provision and protection.

I was so proud of my eight-year-old Trevor the day he wildly kicked a ball on the elementary school playground. The errant ball soared across the playground and hit a teacher in the head. He could have easily slipped into the crowd and remained anonymous. Instead, he made his way over to the teacher to make sure she was all right and to let her know that he was the one who had kicked the ball. I felt a small moment of victory that day, not because of the impressive kick, but because he accepted responsibility for his actions. I encouraged him with, "Great job, Trevor. Now keep doing that for the rest of your life!"

A real man accepts the responsibilities that are right in front of him, big or small. And maybe he even takes responsibility for the greater good of his community as well. What are the needs of the community where you reside? Roll up your sleeves and begin to make a difference. A real man embraces responsibility rather than runs from it.

Pillar 2: He Leads Courageously

We desperately need a generation of men to lead courageously, wherever they are. Your family, your community, and the world are at greater risk when men are weak and when they shrink away from the battles that need to be fought. In his book *Warfighting*, A.M. Gray quoted: "Courage is not the absence of fear, rather it is the strength to overcome fear."[1]

There is a great need for strength right in front of us, every single day. A passive man creates a gap for men with poor intentions to fill. A real man rises up and leads courageously, wherever he is. Sometimes this is unpopular, and sometimes it's even dangerous. Think big rather than small. Choose a battle to be won that is bigger than yourself. This will energize you, spark your imagination, and it will inspire other good men to act. The world needs great leaders right now, and the world is hungry for courageous men to follow. In *Braveheart*, William Wallace inspires and challenges the local leadership by saying, "Your title gives you claim to the throne of our country, but men don't follow titles, they follow courage ... And if you would just lead them to freedom, they'd follow you."[2]

Yes! Men follow courage. We know it when we see it. We aspire to embody it. We are impacted when we are in its presence, and we are inspired when we encounter it. Be a strong and courageous leader right where you are, men. Your family and the world need you! That is what we wanted our young boys to know long before they became men.

For "Exhibit A" of uncommon and extravagant courage, look up the story of Kyle Carpenter, a member of the United States Marine Corps. He received the Medal of Honor, which is our nation's highest award for valor, courage, and bravery. In short, while deployed in enemy territory and with only seconds to respond, Kyle jumped on a live grenade to protect his fellow soldier who was just a few feet away from it. Amazingly, Kyle survived the blast and lived to talk about it. Not many of us will ever have such an extreme opportunity to demonstrate prolific courage, but all of us can be courageous each and every day.

Pillar 3: He Lives a Life of Service
A real man lives a life of serving others. A toxic, weak man spends his time, energy, and resources building the kingdom of self. Selfish men are greedy and of little benefit to anyone. The world is not a better place when men are consumed with their own power, position, and pride. We need a generation of men who will lead by example and serve the needy of this world.

God knows there is no shortage of needs to be met. A real man lives a life of service and gives his life away! He starts by doing this in his family, and then he goes outward from there. What a testimony our sons' marriages would eventually be if they were known for loving and serving their wives and children in sacrificial and extraordinary ways! What a world this would be if we could get enough men living that way.

Pillar 4: He Understands That <u>WHO He Is</u> Is More Important Than <u>WHAT He Does</u>.

A real man is not caught up in the external land mines of building his career and accumulating great wealth. Of course, there is nothing wrong with building a great career full of monetary gain. However, there are also plenty of ways to get derailed in that process. We see entertainers, athletes, and politicians become consumed by these pursuits and failing on a regular basis. A real man is clear about the fact that his worth and value to this world is not solely dependent upon his outward performance. Likewise, a man's failure does not define him either. The great Winston Churchill framed it this way when he said, "Success is not final, failure is not fatal: It is the courage to continue that counts."

A real man knows he has something important and lasting to offer this world that is not dependent upon his outward success or failure. He has inherent strength and power that compels him to not seek his identity in his work or his success. *He* is the gift that will change the world, not his talents and his accomplishments.

Sometimes a successful man can get consumed with always needing more. Not to mention the artificial and temporary flattery that often accompanies great achievements. He is tempted to lose sight of what is most important and lasting. Geoff, Ronnie, and I wanted our boys to know that they were valued and loved regardless of the path they chose and that we would be there for them no matter what—especially in their failures. Our faith perspective also informed this pillar of manhood. We wanted our boys to know that their identity is in an unchanging God rather than the artificial and temporary applause of this world.

Those were our four pillars of manhood. We defined a man living out *authentic* masculinity as one who was practicing these four pillars. We had lots of great discussion for years around each one of these tenants. We drilled our boys over and over, and we even made plaques to hang on their walls. We built the precepts of manhood on these four tent-posts and repeated them over and over. We identified our theme, verse 2 Timothy 4:7-8, and off we went!

What is your definition of a man? I encourage you to take some time and thoughtfully come up with your own working definition. Do this, especially if you are currently raising a young man in your home. Give him the gift of clarity as to what a real man IS so that he can recognize what a real man isn't—the counterfeit. You will cherish these conversations, and he will be better for it. More importantly, you'll be doing your part in helping this world become a better place by raising a positive, powerful, authentic young man. Your future daughter-in-law and your grandkids will thank you for raising a man who will positively impact their lives and even the world.

Part 2
The Big Three

Who are the buyers?
Who are the traffickers?
Who are the victims?

I think it is important to recognize a few things—yes, it CAN happen to anybody, but the reality is there are groups of people who are at higher risk that end up in any of these categories: victims, buyers, and sellers. If you identify as female, have experienced a high level of adverse childhood experiences, are from a marginalized people group, and have been desensitized to abuse as a child or young adult then, you are more at-risk than others. Similarly, if you identify as male and have the same vulnerabilities as listed above, your rate of getting caught up in drugs, gangs, pimping, and organized crime increases. Studies show that the majority of buyers are 35–55-year-old Caucasian men with expendable income who have also been exposed to pornography or have a pornographic addiction. Does that mean we stereotype and assume the worst of people? Of course not! But we can utilize research to build in prevention tools for our vulnerable boys and girls at an early age to prevent the buying and selling and decrease rates of victimization.

Rebecca Bender
CEO and founder of the Rebecca Bender Initiative
Author of *In Pursuit of Love* and *Roadmap to Redemption*

"There are a thousand hacking at the branches of evil to one who is striking at the root."

Henry David Thoreau

5

The Buyers

Who Are the Buyers?

What does the typical sex buyer look like? What is he thinking? Why is he doing this? Who is he?

When I first started looking into the subject of child trafficking, the first and biggest conundrum I found myself in was trying to understand who in the world is buying children to have sex with them? I mean, seriously... I get the concept of an extramarital affair. It happens all the time. I get someone at work who succumbs to an advance from a co-worker. I can understand the whispered lie of pornography and its addictive nature pulling guys down a dark path, convincing them it's harmless and that there are no victims. All of the above are prevalent and not surprising in today's oversexualized culture.

But, a child? Someone as young as nine, ten, or eleven years old? I'll spare you the details of things I know of involving even younger kids than that. To share those details here would be largely unproductive. While exploring the truly dark issues surrounding extremely young victims is necessary and worthwhile, we'll save that for another day. My brain goes into overdrive trying to figure out what has gone wrong in someone's life where the buying of a child for sex is even a remote possibility. Or for that matter, buying someone of ANY age. Research shows that the most searched word on the Internet when looking for porn is the word "teen." Research also shows that if you are willing to look at child pornography, then you are likely to engage in sexual acts with children. They actually go hand in hand. To actually act on purchasing a child to have sex with is beyond understandable to me. To have some form of a sexual encounter with youth in their adolescence is perplexing, to say the least.

During my time with Saving Innocence, I have become friends with Sarah Godoy. Sarah has her master's in social welfare, and she has been a research associate at the UCLA Jane and Terry Semel Institute for Neuroscience and Human Behavior. As if all that isn't enough, she is currently enrolled in a PhD program for social work. I talked with her about buyers, and she informed me that in 2015, federal legislation demarcated traffickers and purchasers of sex as equally culpable, though we don't treat them as such. We continue to use euphemisms like "John" to describe purchasers of sex when we should identify them as a sex buyer or child rapist.

And Sarah is right! Why is it that an adult male raping a child while thrusting himself on her in a deviant, oftentimes violent, sexual way called a "John?" I have friends named "John." I go to the bathroom in a "John." A girl sending a breakup letter to her boyfriend sends him a "Dear John" letter. Yet, a man raping a child is called a "John." Sounds a bit ridiculous, doesn't it?

Language Is Important

Language is important because it sets the table for our conversations and conveys common understanding. Like many other advocates in the anti-human sex trafficking field, I propose that "John" is an outdated term based on an outdated understanding of a misunderstood crime. The term "John" was originally used by the purchaser to maintain his anonymity. If we continue to use this term, in effect, we are helping this crime remain in hiding, which is the exact opposite of what should be happening. In those same conversations, you might even hear someone refer to one of the victims as a "child prostitute." NO!!! There is actually no such thing as a "child prostitute." Let's NEVER allow the term prostitute to be used when labeling a victim of child abuse. And while we're at it, can we please stop referring to child victims as "underage women!?" They are not underage women—they are children, kids, minors! And finally, let's start right now calling the buyer exactly that—"a sex buyer," or a "child rapist," as Sarah suggests.

In this book, we will not take a deep dive into the complex psychology of a pedophile or a rapist. There are plenty of resources out there written by well-respected experts in those fields who do a deeper dive into all this than I will. We'll stay a little broader in our examination of the sex buyer. There are several variations of the common sex buyer that we'll consider. For the purposes of this book, I would like to focus on the majority of sex buyers who are otherwise just "regular guys." Below is a collage of profiles and perspectives from experts in the field that provide a basic understanding of who these buyers are.

The Regular Guy

The majority of sex buyers are what I would like to describe as "The Regular Guy." He is otherwise going about his normal, everyday life pursuing his career and oftentimes raising a family. The odds are high that you know someone who buys sex in one form or another. I'll bet you would be surprised to find out who it is. I had an interesting conversation with my friend and former board member of Saving Innocence Michelle Talley. Michelle is a licensed clinical social worker and faculty at UCLA's Department of Social Welfare. She told me that many of these guys are regular married men with wives and children. They have somehow dreamed up or seen online some kind of deviant sexual behavior that they know their wives would never go for. That leads them to the place where they purchase some time with someone they can have power over, do whatever they want with, and then return to their normal life.

The plot thickens. Notice that Ms. Talley said, "someone they can have power over." That is a very interesting and revealing choice of words. And yet, it makes so much sense. This crime has everything to do with power and money. It's no wonder so many of the buyers are white suburban males and so many of the victims are young girls of color. In the ten-year history of Saving Innocence, serving nearly 2,000 youth ranging from ages 7 to 21, approximately 80 percent of our historical client pool have been minorities. Sixty percent of these kids are African American, and 20 percent are Hispanic. This speaks to systemic and societal issues of racism and oppression, not to mention the fundamental breakdown of the family. The national conversation regarding systemic racism and injustice is at an all-time high, and all of those issues come to light via human trafficking. It's no coincidence that human trafficking is often referred to as "Modern-Day Slavery."

Sting Operation
In my time at Saving Innocence, I have become friends with Captain Kent Wegener. He is a 30-plus year veteran of the Los Angeles County Sheriff's Department and is the former head of the Human Trafficking Task Force. He has had a front-row seat to thousands of sex buyers through his role of enforcing the pertinent laws. Captain Wegener backs up what Michelle Talley just said by saying, "There are those that perpetuate their deviant sexual desires by using commercial sex because their fetishes or deviant lust have no place in a normal relationship and would never be tolerated or accepted by a traditional spouse."

We know that these buyers come from all walks of life. Contained in the bucket of sex buyers are doctors, lawyers, dentists, little league coaches, pastors, cops, neighbors, and relatives, many of whom look just like the guy next door. And perhaps might actually BE the guy next door! I live in a sleepy, suburban part of Los Angeles County, about an hour north of downtown. We are best known for the amusement park in our town. I found out we are also known for something else.

One day, I had a meeting with the LA County Sheriff's Department Human Trafficking Task Force. Captain Wegener let me know that in my little suburban town north of downtown Los Angeles they had recently put an advertisement online offering a minor to have sex with as part of a sting operation. He told me that within two hours, they had several hundred hits on the ad. I now look at my neighbors differently. When my wife and I are out to dinner, I look around me and wonder if any of those guys are dining with me. This is NOT only an inner-city problem. This is a problem experienced in every zip code and a problem with humanity everywhere. Sadly, it is perpetuated primarily by men.

I had a fascinating experience when Captain Wegener invited me to join him on a ride along during a sting operation they were conducting in an undisclosed part of Los Angeles. I sat in a blacked-out undercover car watching buyer after buyer stop and proposition a decoy. One after the other, men were handcuffed, fingerprinted, photographed, and taken to jail. In an instant, their lives were forever changed.

Those guys did not know we were going to be there that night. Buying sex on their way home was a spur-of-the-moment decision when they saw the opportunity. While it's possible this was the first time for some, I'm guessing many, if not most, of these men were actively looking for the opportunity to prey upon vulnerable women. The "regular guy" was on his way home from work, and for many, home to be with his family. He chose to indulge his animalistic nature and pulled over to act on his undisciplined sexual urges. I'm hoping that an unplanned night in jail along with $10,000 in court fees accompanied with a dash of embarrassment is enough to prevent him from repeating this offense. But my fear is that it will take more than that to get his attention. I'll never forget the look on some of these men's faces when they were being held in a glassed-in room during their processing. Sad, dejected, motionless, and maybe a little embarrassed. My look on them was a mixture of curiosity, anger, and sadness. I wondered what had gone wrong in their life that had led them to the place of purchasing some kind of sexual encounter on the street from a complete stranger.

My friend, former colleague, and child sex trafficking survivor Oree Freeman recalls this: "Oftentimes, when I was finishing up in a motel room with a guy, he would start talking about going home to his wife and kids. Kids who were oftentimes the same age as I was." The allure of purchasing sex can be overpowering for some. In some cases, the "regular guy" might even be a pastor on his way to lead a Christmas Eve service at his church. Such a man went on the record in the documentary *Sex + Money: A National Search for Human Worth*. He said:

I had fantasized about sex with somebody other than my wife through pornography. Now I was living the fantasy, except the actual experience didn't match the illusion at all. But, there was enough pleasure along with this cocktail of shame and self-hatred and guilt. The worst part of that night for me, worse than looking into the trusted face of my wife and kids on the holiest of nights, worse than all of that, was the knowledge that I was going to do it again.[3]

This particular encounter was not with a minor; however, he also said that he had spent an estimated $300,000 purchasing sex when he was actively addicted.

The Sports Fan
A subset of the "regular guy" is the "sports fan." We know that whenever large groups of men are gathered, human trafficking is present. You may have heard that the Super Bowl is the biggest day of the year for human trafficking. And it might be. But sex trafficking is happening every day of the

year—whether it's a major sporting event, a trade show, or just a regular night out with the boys. There seems to be a small percentage of men who work the purchasing of sex into their evening's entertainment, and oftentimes, that translates both knowingly and unknowingly into purchasing minors.

The number of crisis intervention calls in our work in Los Angeles spiked when the World Series was in town. It's nauseating to me that something meant for good in a city is used for child abuse in the form of child sex trafficking. In my recent meeting with executives from the Los Angeles Rams football franchise, I said that when I heard the NFL was coming back to LA, I was both excited and concerned. I let them know that the beautiful new stadium they built in Inglewood will be a disaster in the lives of children in Los Angeles. I proposed a partnership between the Rams and those in the city fighting against child trafficking. Recently, the NBA All-Star Game was in Los Angeles. The case managers at Saving Innocence are in touch with minors who were showing them fistfuls of money earned from their nights of "work" near the Staples Center around the time when the NBA was in town.

What sports teams and venues are you near? My call to action is not just to the Rams, but to every sports franchise in America and every entity that owns the venues where they play. I let the Rams executives know that, through no fault of their own and through completely unintended consequences of their incredible product, they were unknowingly contributing to the environment that enables human trafficking. If we can have these important conversations, then let's show these athletes and executives how they can be proactive partners in the solution.

Rachel Thomas, whom you met in Chapter 3, as well as Harmony Dust Grillo, whom you'll hear from later in the book, are survivors who have partnered with Major League Baseball in their "Strike Out Slavery" campaign in stadiums around the country. Major League Baseball All-Star Albert Pujols and his wife, Deidre, have been instrumental in making this important movement happen in ballparks after baseball games. This is a great first step by MLB. Now, let's see if the NFL can take it to the next level! How about you too, NBA?

Having an intentional awareness effort lead by professional sports teams would be a great PR move, at the very least, and at most, we would see fewer kids trafficked if we tightened things up around our sports venues. I'd love to speak with teams and athletes about how they can join this fight!

My co-author, Jessica, says this about her time in "the life" as related to sporting events: "I was trafficked in downtown Los Angeles right around the Staples Center on game nights. It was common on game nights, whether a few feet away from the Staples Center or just down the road. I could tell that half the time, the buyer was acting on a whim. I would call him a "situational abuser." For a situational abuser, it doesn't matter if their victim is thirteen or thirty."

As you learned in Chapter 2, Jessica has substantial lived experience with all kinds of buyers over a long period of time. She has almost literally seen it all. I asked Jessica to describe and define what a buyer looks like from her firsthand experience. We are honored to have her voice contributing so generously in this book because she is a bona fide expert, and we can trust what she says on this topic because of her extensive personal experience.

Jessica says, "The buyers are anywhere from young teens to older, more experienced men and can also be women too. The young men or teens usually are very curious about buying a girl who is being sold for sex. They have heard and learned from an early age that it can be a cool thing to have experienced an encounter with someone that is being exploited. They were under the impression that the victims are excited by the thought of having sex with different people. The purchasers also believe that when they pay money to the victim, they can do whatever they want to them. This is also true for the older and more experienced buyer."

The idea of "power" that Michelle Talley mentioned is revisiting us here again. The buyers think that because they put down some money, they are now entitled to do whatever they want.

Jessica continued: "There have been instances when a buyer has paid a victim to perform a particular act and instead has forced her to endure various forms of torture along with the initial rape. She has had to agree to it in order to please her trafficker. Most, if not all, purchasers think that the victim they are purchasing is not human but merely a thing to purchase, abuse, and discard when they are done. Some buyers think because a victim is in the situation they are in that no one cares for or loves them so nobody would ever think to look for them."

Jessica is using some very powerful words and phrases in her descriptions of the common sex buyer and these encounters. Words like torture, rape, not human, a thing, abuse, and discard are all packed with explosive imagery. When she was telling me this, I pressed her for a little more on the word torture. That was very intriguing to me because the idea of "torture" seems to add another layer to this crime that most people have not considered. She declined to go into much detail, and I respectfully agreed that this book is not really the place for that. While these encounters are not always physically violent, Jessica is informing us of the deep pain associated with someone buying sex and their victim.

Jessica went on to share more about who the buyers are and what they look like. She said, "I have seen buyers as young as twelve years old riding a bike and as old as ninety. However, most are between the ages of thirty and sixty. One time I had a father-son duo. It was sort of like a rite of passage that the father provided for his son."

And here I was, providing my son with pitching lessons, football camps, and math tutors. What was I thinking?

Jessica said, "My lived experience tells me that about forty percent of the buyers are white suburban males, forty percent Hispanic, and twenty percent all others. At least that was true for me where I was working in Los Angeles at the time. If the victim is black, she is not allowed to date a black buyer. The pimp feels threatened by a black customer and fears he will lose his property. About half of the buyers are otherwise pretty normal with nice cars, nice houses, and a nice life. Of those I would consider normal, they would often take me out to dinner and engage in conversation. Many of these were repeat customers. One time, I knew a firefighter who acted like my boyfriend. We even argued like a boyfriend and girlfriend. One time, he was going to be out of town for a while, and he dropped off some money for me without even having a date.

"About half of the buyers I would consider pretty weird. Most of these men resorted to buying sex because they couldn't get a traditional partner in the traditional ways.

One time, I had a widower who wanted me to dress like his deceased wife and sleep in his wife's robe in their bed. He used me to relive the feelings of his lost wife. Kind of sad, really. In my experience, many of the buyers were not malicious and meant me no harm. They were just hurt, lonely men who wanted some form of intimacy. Intimacy that apparently, they were unable to achieve in traditional ways.

"I'll spare you the details of the other crazy stuff and the weird fetishes I encountered when I was in the life. Just know that there are some hurting, messed up people out there who are living a damaging fantasy life. We'll leave it there for now."

We owe Jessica our deepest gratitude for sharing these sensitive parts of her past life with us and providing an invaluable resource to help us understand what is really going on out there.

Special Agent Ryan Dalton
In the process of writing this book, I was fortunate to be introduced to Ryan Dalton. His previous day job was as a special agent in the US Department of State. He has a wealth of experience in anti-human trafficking work. I asked Ryan to share what he has seen up close in the way of sex buyers to further round out our expanding discussion.

Ryan clarified things beautifully when he explained, "A buyer is any person who purchases commercial sex. This definition includes lots of people, not just those who exchange money for intercourse. Commercial sex includes paying for sex, paying to enter a strip club, subscribing to a sex cam service, or even phone sex hotlines. Not all of these are illegal, but they all involve purchasing sex in some fashion. Each of these examples involves the same fundamental exchange:

something of value is traded for a sex act. Buyers are people who financially support the sex industry. "In my experience, buyers are not looking for sex. They are looking for intimacy. They are lonely people. Many of them are angry they cannot find a girlfriend, or angry their relationship with their wife isn't how they imagined it would be, or are so busy with work they justify purchasing sex as the most efficient way to meet their need. I am not a psychologist, but I have never been convinced buyers are merely seeking sexual release with a stranger. Buyers are seeking intimacy and they don't know how to find it. A person who purchases sex will never be naked enough.

"Lonely buyers want a human connection, community, and to be fully known and fully loved. Sex is a form of acceptance, even if they have to pay for it and use it to self-medicate an existential emptiness with a band-aid. Buyers also feel entitled to sex, and often you will hear a buyer justify his decision by saying he is getting his needs met. Entitlement, narcissism, and loneliness are dangerous ingredients when mixed together.

"Before I worked for the State Department, I was an attorney specializing in human trafficking law and policy. My primary job was to write laws to be enacted at the state level, and I worked in support of state legislators throughout the US to achieve this. However, I was most active in my home state, Tennessee, and during this career, I wrote twenty-nine laws, which are now enacted. One of these laws enhanced the penalty for purchasing sex. The Tennessee Bureau of Investigation [TBI] does an amazing job of enforcing these laws and aggressively targeting people who are purchasing sex because these talented investigators know sex trafficking is driven by demand. They charge buyers under this enhanced statute to bring the hammer down on the sex trade in Tennessee by prioritizing demand enforcement.

"One TBI-lead sting operation in my hometown resulted in the arrest of forty-two men, one of which, to my family's surprise and shock, was a close family member. I got a call from a friend one Saturday morning to check the newspaper for a name I should recognize. Sure enough, I found a name in an article about the previous night's sting that I immediately knew was my family member. I called the agent in charge of the sting operation, a personal friend of mine, and learned the family member was arrested and charged under a law for which I wrote the penalty enhancement. Fortunately, he did not attempt to buy sex with a minor like other buyers caught during the operation, a crime that carries a much more severe penalty. If I did not work for the State Department, I would have taken a job with the TBI and been one of the arresting agents present during the arrest. This hit too close to home.

"I know buyers are lonely and are looking for genuine intimacy because a buyer is in my family, and he is lonely. He is lonely because his own choices isolate him and hurt other people. I've seen the emotional and relational consequences of buyer behavior over and over again, both personally and professionally. Men from wealthy suburban neighborhoods, with wives and kids, are caught trying to buy sex all the time. The buyers are our neighbors, go to our churches, and are our co-workers. The odds are good you know someone who buys sex.

"The ripple effect of purchasing sex extends well beyond the exchange between the two people engaging in sex. We don't live in a relational vacuum. Buyers drive the industry for commercial sex, and this industry chews up and spits out young women, boys, and girls, many of whom are coerced into soul-mutilating work. Families suffer and are destroyed when the buyer's secret is finally revealed.

"The good news is buyers can be redeemed. Their decisions don't define them forever. They need justice and harsh legal penalties that reflect the seriousness of the harm they do to the vulnerable in society. But they also need people to show them genuine intimacy, and this means knowing them and their faults but loving them anyway. Admittedly, forgiveness is radical, messy, and difficult. However, a key part of defeating the sex trade involves men being known by other men, by their families, and by people who can lift them out of loneliness and walk alongside them toward authentic masculinity."

There Is Hope
Well said, Ryan! I'm so glad he finished by mentioning words like "redeemed" and "forgiveness." We must believe there is hope and healing in our collective futures. We will talk a great deal more about our role as men in snuffing out this crime.

My friend Morgan Perry, co-producer of *Sex + Money: A National Search for Human Worth, Liberated: The New Sexual Revolution,* and *Beyond Fantasy,* filled me in on her findings when interviewing sex buyers for her documentaries. She had a slightly different take from Ryan's.

She said, "I agree with him that many are lonely, but certainly not all, and perhaps not even the majority. In our experience interviewing men who are former or current buyers for our documentary about them, the men weren't isolated because most had wives and children or were in long-term relationships. They were living two lives—real life and fantasy life, and they purchased people for sex because they wanted the fantasy more. They reached a point where the Internet and their imagination weren't enough anymore. They wanted to show up, pay a girl to do whatever they wanted and be whoever they wanted for the night without any strings attached. So, in many ways, we heard the opposite from them. It wasn't about relationship or intimacy at all. It was about their pleasure, and that's it. Their fix. When we asked them if they had known that many of the women were being trafficked and didn't want to be there, would that have changed anything, they said no. No, they would not have cared because they wanted what they came for, and it was all about them. So, our takeaway was not loneliness or connection or intimacy, but rather entitlement, objectification, and sexual gratification."

Morgan is adding another layer here. Her direct findings showed unremorseful men who didn't care about anything but themselves and their own needs. She did not find men craving intimacy, but rather men craving sexual satisfaction at all costs as their primary objective. However, I am confident that no single perspective covers any particular topic in its totality. I think that this could be one of those moments when both are partially true at the same time. Could there be a twisted cocktail of lonely guys lacking intimacy who are so consumed by this desperate longing that they cross over into complete narcissism and control with the underlying need being what is lacking in their own life?

I hope you now have a clearer picture of who these sex buyers are. You heard from academic experts, law enforcement, policy makers, and most importantly, from Jessica, who saw thousands of buyers up close and personal. You heard that the majority of sex buyers are what appear to be regular guys going about their regular lives—whether that is attending a sporting event or simply on their way home from work. Jessica gave us a glimpse inside the mentality of the buyer, and Ryan framed it well by saying, "buyers are not looking for sex. They are looking for intimacy." Ryan is suggesting that there is something much deeper going on beyond the obvious physical encounter. Morgan then tempered Ryan's input with an alternate perspective from her experience. I'm quite certain that elements of both Ryan's and Morgan's perspectives are correct at the same time. I'm sure many men are driven by loneliness, and many others are driven by the physical encounter and the feeling of having power. Intimacy is a powerful concept. True intimacy binds people together at a deep level, and the lack of intimacy can create a gaping hole in one's life, yearning to be filled.

Of the many facets to this crime, there is none more instrumental in the proliferation of sex trafficking than the sex buyer. It is absolutely an economically driven enterprise, and like every thriving business, it needs a steady supply of customers, or it will go out of business. In its simplest form, sex trafficking exists because the demand for it exists. Wipe out the demand for any product, and the product ceases to be available for purchase. And in this case, oftentimes, the product is young children.

"Commonly mistaken for prostitution, sex trafficking is a form of modern-day slavery in which traffickers use violence, threats, lies, debt bondage, and other forms of coercion to compel individuals to engage in commercial sex acts against their will. It exists not just abroad, but here in the United States."

Polaris/National Human Trafficking Hotline Definition[4]

6

The Traffickers

Who Are the Traffickers?

Traffickers, Exploiters, and Pimps: All of these words can be used interchangeably. "Trafficker" is used in the classroom, and "Pimp" is used on the streets.

What does the typical pimp look like? What is their mindset? What are some of the factors that have led them to the place where they become an exploiter? (For a list of typical characteristics, see Appendix C: Warning Signs of Human Trafficking.)

It cannot be overstated just how important the role of the trafficker is to this crime. Without people actively recruiting and trafficking humans, the fastest-growing criminal enterprise in the world falls apart. The trafficker is the critical conduit for this severe form of abuse and sexual assault. The 2018 annual report for the Human Trafficking Institute states it succinctly when it says:

> [M]any anti-trafficking efforts have little to no impact on the trafficker's business model. Instead, they focus on raising awareness, reducing vulnerability, and

caring for survivors. These efforts are essential, but if we don't stop the traffickers, they will keep creating more victims who need more survivor services.[5]

Former Special Agent Ryan Dalton had plenty to say about traffickers. He previously served in the Houston field office and was assigned to the Houston Human Trafficking Task Force, where he was responsible for investigating international human trafficking crimes. He had plenty to say on who these traffickers are from his unique perspective. He said:

"Just like there isn't a look to a typical trafficking victim, there isn't a typical look to a pimp or a trafficker, I use these terms interchangeably. Films and television show pimps with Cadillacs with chrome wheels, big hats, and canes, but this is merely entertainment and a distraction. A pimp is hard to physically identify because a pimp is someone who pimps, and pimping is the act of selling a person for commercial sex, an activity that doesn't require a person to look any particular way. Another common misconception is that only men are pimps, yet many prosecutions have also involved female pimps who trafficked younger females.

"A trafficking offense against a child occurs any time something of value is exchanged for sex with that child. A gang member who sells a child for sex on the Internet is a pimp. A mother who lets her landlord have sex with her little girl in exchange for free rent is a pimp. Sadly, even a trafficking victim who has been victimized so long she acclimates to the life and begins recruiting girls out of the foster care system to be new victims can also be a pimp. Some pimps are physically violent, others rely more on emotional abuse. All of them use manipulative tactics to maintain control of their victims.

"Further, sex traffickers are narcissistic and entrepre-
neurial. They build a business based on their glory and on
the backs of those they exploit. In some communities, being
a successful trafficker comes with the high life, status at night
clubs, fancy cars, and lots of cash. The trafficker isn't making
the money, though. The victims are. All the earnings the girls
make go first to the trafficker, then some earnings are returned
to them based on what the trafficker finds they need to continue working. Haircuts, new clothes, makeup, condoms, alco-
hol, and drugs are paid from the girls' earnings, but out of the
hands of the trafficker who collected and claimed the money
first. It is clear to the victims who is in charge. Further, the
traffickers' control tactics are driven by their desire for glory.
Victims sometimes have the name or logo of their trafficker
tattooed on their body in order to establish they are his or her
property, and in turn, the trafficker can show other traffickers
how big his stable of girls has become.

"Despite being narcissistic, greedy, and often cruel, it is
important to remember traffickers are human. It is easy to say
human traffickers are monsters! To my unending grief, statements like this appear in messaging from nonprofits that rescue victims out of the darkness of sex trafficking because
they affirm our shared humanity is sacred. Yet, if we dehumanize traffickers, we take two steps backward from effectively
combatting human trafficking.

"The first step backward is because we don't look at the
traffickers as human, so we do the same thing to them that
they do to their victims, and the second step backward is
because we are failing to accurately account for the human
motivations for making choices harmful to themselves and
others. The ability to account for how traffickers make these

choices in a measured and objective manner is essential to reversing and undoing the environment that led them to these decisions."

Special Agent Dalton accurately encapsulates the characteristics of and actions taken by traffickers. To advance our understanding of a trafficker, I wanted to go a step further. So I intentionally sought out the perspective of someone who could speak from their lived experience, specifically, a former trafficker.

Coffee with a Pimp

As part of this journey, I am on a quest to better understand and communicate the issues around sex trafficking. I found myself really wanting to understand what goes on inside the mind of a trafficker. The so-called pimp is certainly the main villain of this narrative. And rightfully so, I might add. A huge missing piece of the puzzle in my mind was the pimp, the exploiter, the trafficker. Although I can make some educated guesses, I wanted to know more and to get a firsthand account, if possible.

Not expecting the answer, I asked my friend Sarah Godoy if she happened to know any current or former pimps. To my surprise, she quickly answered, "Yes, there is a guy out of San Diego that I am connected to via social media." She gave me his name, Armand, so I reached out. He quickly accepted my request to connect. I shot back a request to talk over this project I was working on. He immediately responded with, "Sure, anytime. What works for you?" In a few moments, I had a date and a location set for a face-to-face meeting with this former pimp. I wasn't sure what to expect, but my very first interactions with him were immediate, respectful, and helpful.

I arrived at the designated coffee shop early to get situated. I wanted to make sure we were far enough away from other customers so we could have an open and sensitive conversation. As I sat there for some 20 minutes, I wondered how this meeting would go. What would he be like? What is his back story? Would he be every bit the villain that I envision all traffickers to be? My meeting with Armand provided both challenges and surprises for me to chew on.

Challenge #1—Are Pimps Evil?

After the obligatory small talk and greetings, I reminded him of the purpose of our meeting. I had told him over the phone that I was writing a book and would greatly appreciate some conversation with him to learn more of the realities from his perspective and experience. He started out by saying, "I am not evil, and I am not a bad person. Nor was I when I was in the game."

This was a challenge for me right from the beginning. My surprise wasn't that he thought of himself in high regard; my surprise was that he felt it necessary to open our conversation by saying he wasn't evil. Although I wasn't coming into the meeting with any malice toward him, those are the words I have used many times regarding traffickers and their controlling, abusive activity. In fact, in this book, there are places where I will refer to this crime as being "evil." For him to lead with that disclaimer made me think he had heard that description before. He was ready to make his defense even before it was required.

He went on to share more of his story by letting me know about the struggles he endured as a kid. He said that he was born and raised in poverty. His father was verbally and physically abusive and out of his life by age 12. At 12 years old, his family was out on the streets and homeless for two years. During this period, he was lured into the neighborhood gang. It was appealing, welcoming, and gave him a sense of manhood and security. He was heavily influenced by rap music, which at the time was all gangster rap. At 13 years old, his childhood best friend was murdered. At 15, he began to sell marijuana, and all the money he made was turned over to his mom for gas and food for the family. He continuously watched the slightly older generation in his neighborhood either die an early death or go to jail. He felt that to even make it to 18 years of age was a miracle. He told me that his mother became addicted to drugs and had a drug dealer/user boyfriend move into his house. At 16 years old, his friend was shot and killed. His funeral was the first Armand ever attended. This experience left an indelible mark on him that he will never forget as he spoke of kissing the hard, cold forehead of his friend lying in the casket. After sharing more of his childhood with me, he looked me in the eye and said, "I needed to survive."

Survival is such a powerful concept. I have heard young survivors use the same word over and over. They have spoken of having "no choice" and "needing to survive." I found it fascinating that the former trafficker was saying some of the same things that our victims say. This former trafficker talked of needing to survive—a reality no child should ever be faced with.

A 2010 study by researchers at the DePaul University College of Law in Chicago, Illinois, seemed to confirm what Armand was telling me. This study interviewed ex-pimps to discover what the pertinent factors of their behavior were. Their 91-question survey revealed some striking common denominators for a trafficker's childhood. Their study found that 88 percent experienced physical abuse while growing up, 76 percent experienced childhood sexual assault, 88 percent experienced domestic violence in the home, and 84 percent experienced drugs and alcohol abuse in the home.[6] Those are awfully impactful numbers that would definitely shape any child while a dangerous life trajectory is being formed.

Armand went on to describe the mindset and reality of kids in the inner city. He said a young Black kid from the inner city aspires to be a pro athlete or rapper. They don't see any other options. When those don't happen, they have to find other means to survive. Armand said that when he started, there was considered to be nothing wrong with pimping girls. Singers like Snoop Dog and Nelly put out songs making it seem like it was okay. He reminded me that he was totally on his own at age 15 and needed to make money to survive. Law enforcement knew what was happening. He said, "They would ask about guns and drugs and didn't mind that we were rolling with these girls."

Challenge #2—By Choice, not Force
Armand said he had a phrase: "By choice, not force. I never forced any girl to work for me. I used to sit down with girls and write up what we would each do. I kept all the money, but I also paid for her food, shelter, and clothing. I asked, 'Do you want to do this?' There were lots of times when they said no."

What Armand said about this was yet another challenge for me. This was both challenging and surprising to me because we interact with survivors all the time who have experienced extreme violence and force. The 2018 Federal Human Trafficking report put out by the Human Trafficking Institute states that "In 2018, evidence in over half (56.2 percent) of the sex trafficking cases indicated that a defendant used physical violence to force a victim to engage in commercial sex."[7]

I pushed back with Armand on what he had said about not using force, and he replied that "force certainly happens, but just not with me."

Are these thoughts unique to Armand, or is this something all traffickers believe? One thing we know about traffickers is that they lack empathy—you have to in order to sell someone. Did he have a lack of empathy and, therefore, was unable to understand his power and impact? Even if it wasn't physical force, we know that BY DEFINITION, trafficking often includes "manipulation" and "coercion."

My friend and colleague Oree Freeman, a child sex trafficking survivor, directly refutes the idea that these kids are not forced. To be fair, Oree was never associated with Armand, so his reality was different from hers. But according to Oree, "It was never a choice, it's not a choice for these kids. Whether it was an influence or if it was somebody physically forcing them to do it. Whether it was their circumstances, it's not a choice."

Oree continued to describe what her relationship to her trafficker was like by saying that she remembered when "he grabbed me by my hair and dragged me down the street with my knees scraping the ground. My normal was if I didn't make enough money for 'Daddy' and make my quota, I was getting beaten upside my head with a forty-five-millimeter gun. My normal was not eating for two or three days because I didn't make enough money. After all this, he would say things like, 'You want to make me happy, don't you? Don't you want to make Daddy happy?'"

Economics

Armand then shared with me the economics of his business. He said that he could quickly make $1,000 per day and, at his peak, would bring in $20,000 per week. He said that his survival instincts quickly moved to greed. He liked the money and the things he could buy with it. We talked about the lack of options and opportunities for kids in the inner city and how once a kid begins making this kind of money, it's almost impossible to suggest he get a regular job in a fast-food restaurant. We both agreed that it's pretty tough to make an entire paycheck's earnings in one day and then ask the young man to walk away from it.

In a May 18, 2014 article in the Los Angeles Daily News, Christina Villacorte interviewed a different former pimp who wished to remain anonymous. If there was ever any doubt that the crime of human trafficking is motivated by economics, he framed his perspective like this:

"Women are sitting on a gold mine—they got something between their legs that's like a commodity."[8]

Poverty is a driving contributing factor in human trafficking. The significant economic cash flow for the perpetrators cannot be denied. The business model of renting a human being over and over and over is a powerful one. In business terms, it's a "reusable product" with a high profit margin.

The global economic statistics regarding human trafficking profits shockingly confirm what is driving this crime. The 2018 Annual Report for the Human Trafficking Institute states that "all human traffickers raked in over 150 billion dollars in 2018. To put this into perspective, that is greater than the net profits of Microsoft, Apple, Wells Fargo, Samsung, and J.P. Morgan COMBINED."[9]

Challenge #3—They're Willing Participants

This surprise was definitely a challenge for me to wrap my brain around. Armand suggested that "far more women and girls were participating willingly than is commonly accepted." He went on to say that "only the very traumatized girls are doing the talking these days. I have known lots of girls who were voluntarily in the game. They are not speaking out, and so society has lumped them all into the same category. The impression is that every girl being trafficked has been forced and has had violence used against her. While that has certainly happened, there are also lots of girls that are doing this willingly."

Before anyone loses their mind (including me), there is an entire conversation to be had about what manipulation, brainwashing, societal pressures, media messaging, and the lack of an intact family unit has done to these girls. As previously stated, many girls find themselves in survival mode through no fault of their own and are fighting for their very existence. Long before they are ever trafficked, they have been groomed by society for this purpose without even knowing it. Most have already experienced unspeakable sexual abuse before they ever met their pimp. In Chapter 7, "The Victims," you'll learn more about how this works.

I am honored to know Harmony Dust Grillo. She is a trafficking survivor who was exploited primarily through strip clubs. Since then, she has founded and runs an impactful organization called Treasures, which reaches out to those same women trapped in strip clubs. She also authored her life story in *Scars & Stilettos.* When talking about this very topic, she dropped this deep thought on me: "Research shows that eighty-nine percent of women in the commercial sex industry want to leave but don't see any other options. This begs the question, what is choice without options? It's not really a choice if there are no options."

Now that's worth thinking about. At first glance, it might look like she has a choice to stay or run. However, from her perspective, she doesn't see any other options at all. She only sees one "choice," to stay and comply. So, does she actually have a choice when she can see only one option on the table? Beyond the victim's perspective, many live in a community where there are actually fewer available options and potential avenues of escape. There are social and environmental factors that reduce available options, thus creating one more significant barrier to escape.

Challenge #4—A Trafficker Became Human
Maybe the biggest challenge I received that day was not about Armand's experience, perspective, or information. It was the simple fact that the concept of a "pimp, trafficker or exploiter" just became human. He now has a name, a face, and a story. Could it be that he is not the monster I once thought he was? Armand told me that "the same conditions that produce the victim also produces the pimp."

Without ever meeting a trafficker, I knew there had to be a hard story from their childhood. I knew there had to be an element of desperation and need that had fueled their actions. I knew there must have been an element of abuse that they had also encountered. And I also knew that there is a systemic lack of options and opportunities for young kids growing up in our inner cities. It's clear to me that most of these traffickers were set up for failure in their own way. Their early childhood environment pointed them in a particular direction from which the odds were definitely stacked against them.

75

Now I have to grapple with the fact that traffickers are *also* human beings trying to survive, albeit misguided, dark, and painful for many. I came away from my meeting sensing, more than ever before, that part of the solution we are looking for has to include early childhood training and intervention for the vulnerable populations of potential traffickers. It's not just about showing kids all the options though; it's actually about creating new pathways for vulnerable and at-risk youth in communities that operate with deficits. We must work at changing environments so that there are more options. We have to expand their world of opportunities.

I bought Armand an iced coffee and said thank you and goodbye. He offered to stay connected and to help in any way he could moving forward. He left me by saying that he has found his purpose. He said that this part of his life, providing training and awareness to the issues of human trafficking, is the most fulfilling part of his life. You might be interested to know that Armand recently published his book entitled *Raised in Pimp City*. He also runs a great effort in San Diego helping inner-city kids called Paving Great Futures (www.pavinggreat-futures.org). Check them both out.

I'll let Jessica follow up on what Armand just said. As you have already learned, she has a vast knowledge of who these traffickers are and how they operate. Also, you might find it interesting that as I read Armand's words to her, she scowled back with a disapproving and skeptical look. To no surprise, Armand's perspective did not line up with Jessica's lived experience. She states:

"In my experience, the typical trafficker is a boyfriend of sorts. He is someone who is offering protection and provision to vulnerable girls. He offers a false sense of security to a girl who is lacking authentic security. The typical trafficker also plays a father figure role as well. Since most of the girls who are being trafficked are lacking a healthy and present biological father, this plays to his advantage. Each exploiter is seen differently by the different girls he is controlling. This is usually because he often treats his girls differently. One he may treat more like a girlfriend, and another he treats more like a piece of property. He is a master manipulator who is willing to do anything possible to keep his girls making money for him. In his eyes, we are not seen as human beings with a heartbeat or a pulse. His insidious actions know no limit.

"A common practice of the pimp is creating an emotional and spiritual bond with his victim. For example, it is not uncommon for the trafficker, while having sex with his victim, to whisper in her ear how much he loves her and how beautiful she is. During this time of physical intimacy, he is letting her know how much she is loved and wanted. These are all the things she is longing to hear and experience. Simultaneously, while in the act, he lets her know that she is never allowed to leave him. He whispers, 'If you leave me, I will kill you.'"

When Jessica told me this, my blood began to boil. How dare they take something meant to be so beautiful and unifying and use it as a weapon of manipulation.

To finish this chapter, I would like to bring back Captain Kent Wegener. He is a 30-year veteran of the Los Angeles County Sheriff's Department. I was honored to work with him during his stint as the head of the Human Trafficking Task Force in Los Angeles. He has his own unique experience and perspective on the topic. Captain Wegener relayed his personal experience on the matter.

"The exploiters are not that different from other criminals. Motivated by ego, money, and selfishness, it's easier to make money from someone else's abuse than to work for it in a conventional system of employment. Like the victims, the criminals were often raised in a family of dysfunction, where crime, drugs, and criminality were accepted, encouraged, and expected, and money was obtained at the expense of others who were too weak to protest. The value of a woman, a relationship, and familial stability was lost to domination, sexual gratification, and survival as a predator and not prey."

Traffickers, exploiters, or pimps. By any name, they are a picture of brokenness and pain. Not only are they the recipients of brokenness in their early adolescence, but they are now also the facilitator of brokenness and pain to their victims. They are commodifying their victims and playing a crucial role in the marketplace of sexual exploitation. I'm not surprised that Armand has a very different perspective than Jessica and Oree do. We all have our own reality based on the lens we experience life through. I'll let you, the reader, synthesize all this information from these various perspectives in order to form your own opinion.

The whole issue of sex trafficking is the manifestation of a broken society littered with weak-minded males who allow themselves to travel down a dark path. Whether a buyer or a seller, there is plenty of dysfunction to go around. The intent of this book is to bring education and awareness to this issue through real-life participants and then inspire healthy males to act. More than ever, we need healthy males to rise up and make a difference.

While thousands of broken men are busy acting out on their pain, selfishness, and dysfunction, thousands of abuse victims lie struggling in their wake. Sadly, many of these victims are minors and prepubescent children. Let's take a closer look at who they are and how they got there in the next chapter.

My perception of men was that every man bought sex. I also thought that every man had a desire to have sex with a child because that was all I ever knew. Every single day was consumed with just trying to survive.

Oree Freeman

I was raised in a chaotic home in a neighborhood run by gangs and riddled with violence. Beginning at the age of five, my childhood was also marked by sexual abuse at the hands of multiple people.

Harmony Dust Grillo

I felt unwanted, alone and unimportant.

Rebecca Bender

7

The Victims

Who Are the Victims?

Any child is at risk for exploitation, yet there are a host of factors that make certain populations more vulnerable or at risk than others. Young girls are the most highly identified, yet we know there are more young boys being exploited than are currently being counted in the statistics. Because the vast majority of buyers are male, the traditional majority of sex-trafficked youth in our country are young females.

Some of the nuanced questions regarding the girls are these: What was their childhood like growing up? What are some of the factors that create their vulnerability? Why don't they run away from their trafficker? What is their mindset while they are being exploited? What is their relationship with their pimp like? What kind of danger are they in? So many questions, and there is no singular answer that covers it all. It's more complex than we can give adequate time to in this book, yet we'll give it a shot with the help of some knowledgeable friends. (See Appendix C For a list of warning signs of an individual being trafficked.)

I asked my co-author, Jessica, to further describe the mindset of a child being trafficked. Jessica has firsthand experience and knowledge of what child trafficking is all about because she was a child victim of sex trafficking herself and is now a survivor. Additionally, she has spent over ten years working with kids who are still in the life and working hard to get them out. The following comes directly from her personal experience. She enlightened me with some truly heartbreaking realities.

The Mindset

Jessica said, "A child being trafficked becomes paranoid and hyper-vigilant at all-time high levels. She is at risk of being tortured or beaten every single day. She is checking to make sure car doors are unlocked, and she never wears a seatbelt in case things turn dangerous and she has to run. She is constantly in fear of being hurt, raped, or killed. She is constantly having her life threatened. She lives every day with the thought, 'I could die today.' Survival instinct takes over, and she is always thinking, 'I need to survive' twenty-four, seven. She is preparing for her death. She does not feel like a human being, but more like cattle. She is abused, both physically or sexually, or neglected from an early age. She has usually witnessed abuse at an early age. She feels shame and guilt as she is being revictimized over and over. Dad is not present, physically and or emotionally."

What Jessica said is so hard to process—that a child would be forced to live that way and in that mindset. You first met my friend Rachel Thomas in Chapter 3. She once told me that while she was being trafficked, she was also living day-to-day and in fear for her life. She went on to further confirm the survival mode mindset that so many victims speak of. She said, "During this time of my life, my perception of men was that they were predatory. I was most definitely in survival mode, doing whatever I needed to do to stay alive that day."

As a child victim of sex trafficking, the message is sent early in their life, often by the people closest to them, that their value and human worth are negligible, and in fact, they are disposable. More accurately, they have been taught that the bulk of their value comes from their sexual being because they have been violated by so many at such a young age. Their perceived value is literally coming from the price someone is willing to pay for their sexual activity. Many have come to believe that sexual activity is all they are good for, and that is all they'll ever be used and known for.

My friend Nola Brantley, a nationally known survivor leader and trainer extraordinaire, recently told me this regarding her time in the life years ago: "I thought sex was the most valuable thing I had to offer this world. I thought I was put on this earth to satisfy people sexually."

Living through all of the physical and emotional abuse that Jessica described would be horrendous for anyone of any age. But please keep in mind that we are mainly talking about children here—that the average age of entry is just 12 years old! This is important to note because children at an early age have fewer defense mechanisms, a still-developing physiology, and a fragile emotional state as they work to comprehend all that is happening to them.

A Day in "The Life"
Jessica continued to further elaborate on what these kids are going through on a daily basis by sharing more of her

personal experience. "Here is what my typical workflow looked like when I was active in the life. Many girls today have a similar setup. They will work three full days, and then they will get a break. A break consists of only having to work a half day. So, they basically have a seventy-two-hour shift before they get their break of getting a half day off. This goes on year-round, three hundred sixty-five days per year. I usually had five to ten customers each day for sure. However, oftentimes I had between ten to twenty-five purchasers in one day. The day was not measured in the number of customers but by the amount of cash I brought in. I usually had a quota I was expected to bring in each day."

I remember being so confused when Jessica first described this to me. You mean, you never even had a day off? A "break" was only having to work a half day? A full day could mean as many as 25 different men on any given day? All of this is sobering when you stop and consider it.

There are many other factors that contribute to the exploitation of children in our country. One of them is when a child becomes unsafe at home, they are usually entered into the foster care system. Sadly, a huge percentage of kids being trafficked are from the foster care system. The very infrastructure that is meant to protect them oftentimes fails in that endeavor. Below are some thoughts about what is happening there.

Foster Kids

Here is what we know for sure about foster youth: In order to be placed in the system, they have already had their lives blown up in a myriad of ways. Long before the reality of sex trafficking rears its ugly head, they have experienced all kinds of neglect or abuse. Oftentimes, the trauma of physical and sexual abuse as a very young child has already left its indelible imprint on their heart, mind, and soul.

As a foster youth, their desire for love and attention is peaking because, for many, it has been denied thus far. Not only do they feel the deep human desire for connection, love, and attention, but they also have a very real need for tangible support such as food and shelter. Not to mention the dreams of a future with their own life and family. The typical life lived by a foster youth has all but destroyed his or her self-confidence because all these dreams appear to be unattainable.

The average foster youth moves from place to place, changing locations some seven times by the time they are age 18. A foster kid will typically not say where they "live," but rather where they "stay." They've learned that wherever they happen to be at the time is, by nature, temporary. The vulnerabilities of a foster youth are present, obvious, and in no short supply.

In her May 3rd, 2018, article, "Without family, US children in foster care prey for human traffickers," appearing for the Thomas Reuters Foundation, Ellen Wulfhorst adds this to our conversation by quoting Dorchen Leidholdt, legal center director at Sanctuary for Families, which advocates for domestic violence and sex trafficking survivors:

> Hundreds of thousands of US children live in foster care, prey to predator sex traffickers who may find their young victims at bus stops, shopping malls or street corners as well as on social media and online chat rooms. Often removed from abusive or negligent families, girls and boys in foster care are at high risk.

Traffickers go for our most vulnerable, and kids who are or were in foster care are the most vulnerable children in our society. These predators know all the signs and look for them. Traffickers can tell that 'you're the kid who doesn't have any family.'[10]

Sarah Godoy then added to this narrative, stating the fact that:

The majority of sex trafficked girls (upward of 80 percent) come from the juvenile justice and child welfare systems, creating further vulnerabilities. Though these systems are charged with providing care, many youth lack consistent guardian oversight, steady relationships, and housing stability. One of the most common antecedents to sex trafficking is childhood maltreatment, including sexual abuse. Childhood maltreatment distorts one's view of themselves and others. Sexual abuse has a lasting mental and physical health effect on youth, distorting their understanding of appropriate boundaries and healthy relationships.[11]

In 2013, the Administration for Children and Families reviewed statistics from several studies and found that up to 90 percent of children who were victims of sex trafficking had been involved with child welfare services, which include foster care.[12]

They're easy targets. As one trafficker puts it, "When they go missing, no one is looking for them." Today, the foster care system makes up one of the greatest "supply chains" into human trafficking in our country.[13]

And one survivor, quoted in the O. L. Pathy Foundation report, explicitly expresses this:

> Being in foster care was the perfect training for commercial sexual exploitation. I was used to being moved without warning, without any say, not knowing where I was going or whether I was allowed to pack my clothes. After years in foster care, I didn't think anyone would want to take care of me unless they were paid. So, when my pimp expected me to make money to support 'the family,' it made sense to me.[14]

However, it would be a big mistake if parents let their guard down after reading the above statements stating that some 80-90 percent of trafficked youth are coming out of the foster system. There is an important nuance to be considered. The mistake would be assuming that since your child is at home and not in foster care, that they are safe from predators and exploiters. Where I live and work in anti-trafficking efforts in Los Angeles, the county data states that 70 percent of trafficked youth have their first recovery or disclosure to sex trafficking while they are still at home. Many of these kids soon after find themselves in the child welfare system and continue to be trafficked until we can all work together to help them out. The bottom line is that kids anywhere can be at risk, so everyone has to keep their eyes open.

Manipulation

These vulnerabilities are easily spotted by a predator looking to control a young child via human trafficking. A typical scenario is that in the middle of all these vulnerabilities, a slightly older male who masquerades as a would-be boyfriend walks in. It is noteworthy that oftentimes, the trafficker is decades older and presents as more of a father figure. He gives her all that she is longing for, including the counterfeit love she mistakes for authentic. She loves him in return, and before she knows it, she is caught emotionally, if not physically, in a web of deception, manipulation, and exploitation.

Rachel Thomas said, "Girls who come from broken homes are told, 'You don't have a daddy, I'm the only man who's ever going to look out for you, so you better stick with me.' It's all about manipulation and breaking down a girl's self-esteem so they do what the pimp tells them to do."

In order to further coerce and manipulate the child victim, the trafficker will not hesitate to wield the significant and growing influence he has been working hard to achieve. It is not beyond him to say just the right thing that will seal the deal with his young target. A trafficker might say to their victim, "If you love me, then you'll do this. We need to make money so we can have a life together."

And this particular child who has largely been denied a discernable love will absolutely do what he suggests, working hard to let him know that he has her love and is hoping to earn his in return. The trafficker is an expert at telling her the things she's always wanted to hear, which he uses to manipulate her into doing exactly what he wants. And then he is likely to slip in something like this during a moment of intimacy: "If you ever leave me, I will kill you."

Before long, she has been groomed to carry out his business plan and to do exactly what he had envisioned for her, which is far from what she had envisioned for her own life. She is not sure how she got there, and she has no idea how to get out. And what's worse, youth who go missing from care may never be recovered. The sad reality is that for many minors being trafficked, this is not the worst thing that has happened to them thus far in their life. Jessica spoke painfully about this reality in Chapter 2 when she spoke of the trauma she had experienced during her own childhood adolescence long before she was ever trafficked. We hear this recurring theme over and over from our young survivors.

Many of the kids we work with are so brainwashed and manipulated, they wouldn't even describe themselves as being trafficked or mistreated even when they are in the middle of it. An advocate once told me about a conversation she had with her young client. The client said that she didn't understand why her boyfriend (trafficker) would try to drown her when he had said that he loved her. What an opportunity we have to deconstruct the lies and manipulation she has received and to begin talking about real, authentic love and what healthy relationships look like.

Normalizing the Abnormal

I have had the distinct honor of working with Oree Freeman. Oree is a child trafficking survivor (and so much more) whom I have been privileged to know and work with. She was trafficked from age 11 to 15. She has gone on record as saying that she was "forced to sleep with between seven and fifteen men every single night" throughout those years. Shockingly, she went on to say that "By the time I was twelve years old, I had already been raped four thousand times."

She is one of the strongest, bravest, and most resilient humans I know. Besides that, she is most definitely the life of any party and will keep the room entertained for hours. Similar to Jessica, Oree is an expert on this topic due to her substantial lived experience.

I am grateful to Oree for sharing some of her story and her ability to further illuminate what is happening with these young girls and how they find themselves being trafficked. Below, Oree lays out some of her experiences and what happens to be a fairly typical story for many of the kids who are being sexually exploited in our country.

According to Oree, "A lot of stuff in my childhood became normal. It became okay and normal for an adult male to touch me. And to touch me in ways I didn't understand. It became okay because that's what I was used to. At a very early age, that was what I started to learn as the way you receive love. This is what it feels like when someone cares about you and shows you attention."

Oree is letting us in on some very important clues as to how these girls become so vulnerable and available to their traffickers. We have heard over and over and right here again from Oree that sexual abuse begins at a young age for these kids. Long before their trafficker ever enters the picture, inappropriate touching becomes normal, and what most people would consider abuse has become normalized. Inappropriate touching simply becomes *not that big of a deal,* which inches them closer to full-blown sexual exploitation. A gradual expanding of boundaries relaxes the defense systems and dulls the adverse reactions that most of us would immediately feel. And one step at a time, the unthinkable happens. A child moves ever closer to becoming available to those with horrible intentions for their lives.

Like so many of these child victims, Oree was being groomed for commercial sexual exploitation from the age of eight when those close to her were beginning to sexually abuse her before she even understood what was happening. Those close to her, who should have been protecting her and modeling healthy love for her, were instead doing the exact opposite. This damaged her young perception of who she was and what was normal to expect from men. At age 11, she ran away from home, which led her straight into the arms of a trafficker who was ready to prey on these vulnerabilities. At Saving Innocence, we see Oree's story repeated over and over in far too many victims.

Special Agent Ryan Dalton adds this from his professional observations on the victims he has experienced from his law enforcement perspective:

"A middle school girl with low self-esteem who is told she is pretty for the first time will want more positive attention. A child who never had an involved father and is moved between foster homes for most of his or her youth will be more likely to follow an older stranger who tells them he loves them and will take care of them. Traffickers exploit the desire of a child to be loved, to belong, and to be accepted.

"Desire for belonging is powerful and can be easily exploited by the cunning. This is the reason victims don't merely run away from their traffickers. Victims are subjected to a cycle of abuse where in one moment they may be brutally beaten and in the next moment told they are special and part of a family. Over time, this behavior is reinforced so frequently it creates a trauma bond to the trafficker.

"Victims who experience this strong emotional attachment to their abuser are not likely to merely run away because they see this abuser as a person who loves them. The victim is captured in his or her mind because the victim is brainwashed, and brainwashing is a far more effective and stronger prison than physical shackles. Besides, where would the child go? Where is safe to run to? Who can be trusted? For a child victim, the sometimes violent, sometimes loving known is better than attempting to run to the entirely unknown."

Neuroscience
I came across an important article that helps further explain how all of this fits together with children. We can gain some important scientific clues from an article by Lily Dayton found in the May 2nd, 2018, edition of the *Pacific Standard,* entitled "How Neuroscience can help us treat trafficked youth." In her article, she says:

> A common misconception is that these youths are choosing to engage in the commercial sex trade. But as recent advances in neuroimaging techniques help scientists unravel the myriad ways that trauma affects the brain, emerging evidence suggests that brain changes resulting from trauma could make young people more vulnerable to exploiters and less receptive to people trying to help. Rather than making a conscious decision to rebel, these kids are simply doing their best to survive, using the adaptive strategies that their brains developed in response to a perilous world. Survival is the brain's top priority. Young people growing up in dangerous environments will develop brains that are highly responsive to threat cues.[15]

Survival is such a powerful concept. According to Jessica and Oree, as well as the available emerging neuroscience, these kids who are being trafficked have been thrust into daily situations where their very survival is at stake and they are responding as such. This trauma has rewired their brain and fueled their every decision.

Why Didn't You Just Leave?

You might be thinking what so many people immediately think when they hear these stories. Why don't they just leave? There are so many psychological and emotional entanglements to address. We can start with the Stockholm syndrome. Stockholm syndrome is a psychological response. It occurs when hostages or abuse victims bond with their captors or abusers. This psychological connection develops over the course of the days, weeks, months, or even years of captivity or abuse. Jessica has stated that "the abuse of the known is better than what is unknown, and therefore bonding and remaining with an abuser is more favorable than running into the unknown."

Many trafficking victims simply give up because they see no way out. And of course, there is the real threat of violence should they attempt to get out and fail in that attempt. Rachel Thomas spoke convincingly of this in chapter 3. She got to the point where she determined that her only escape from this life was to actually take her own life. Thankfully, she failed in her attempt.

Rebecca Bender is a nationally known survivor leader, trainer, and founder of the Rebecca Bender Initiative. She is on a lifelong quest to provide training, awareness, and tools for survivors and their recovery. More than that, she is someone I consider a friend and whom I deeply respect. In one of her training pieces, she recently posted this concerning this very question. Her answer will further enlighten us on the predicament at hand. Rebecca's post said:

My parent's divorced when I was 9 and it was a messy divorce—that created a lot of vulnerabilities in my heart. I felt unwanted, alone and unimportant. After high school, I had my daughter and started going to community college. Let me tell you, 21 years ago there was not the support or acceptance there is today for single moms in school. Those old vulnerabilities of being alone and unimportant resurfaced. Until I met the most amazing guy. He was charming, thoughtful, and made time for my daughter and me. After a whirlwind 6-month relationship, I thought I was in love and ready to move with him to Vegas to build a life together. I realized within 24 hours of us arriving in Vegas he was not the man he said he was.

So this is the question that comes up next for everyone: Why didn't you leave? That is a normal question for a healthy adult brain to ask. But, what I think people don't realize is as survivors of trafficking, we are growing up in the same culture as you. I watched the same movies as you. I watched the same TV shows as you. When my situation with my trafficker does not look like those sensational images: a dirty mattress, duct tape and handcuffed to a radiator, I am not identifying as a victim of trafficking because my situation doesn't look like that.

For a long time, I identified as a domestic violence survivor. I thought my boyfriend loves me. He said he is sorry. He said I wouldn't have to do it again tomorrow.

The same power and control cycle domestic violence survivors find themselves in happens in trafficking. The same abuse and honeymoon and lies and apologies. And so ... in the midst of it we're not thinking with healthy adult brains. We're thinking with traumatized, defrauded, abused, in "love" or should I say brainwashed cult-like infatuation, young, vulnerable brains and we're holding that to a sensational image of "trafficking" that doesn't exist.[16]

Rebecca is highlighting a very important idea for us to consider. Those who are on the outside of this problem and trying to figure it out can't understand why these trafficking victims just don't get up and leave. Beyond the very real threat of violence to themselves or their loved ones, Rebecca reminds us that oftentimes, they don't consider themselves as trafficking victims. So how do you leave human trafficking if your perception is that you are not actually in human trafficking? It's a mind-boggling and manipulative cycle of abuse.

Please check out Rebecca's memoir entitled *In Pursuit of love* to learn more.

Whether these kids fall prey to subtle brainwashing and manipulation or to the not-so-subtle tactics of immediate violence and threats, they find themselves stuck with no visible way of escape. They are made to feel broken and threatened by their pimp. Through his controlling and manipulating tactics, they're made to believe that they are damaged goods, and their only value is found in a life of trafficking. Not to mention, in a strange and twisted way, their trafficker is somehow fulfilling their longing for intimate attention and protection. They are yearning for the love they've never had, and he is somehow providing what they think they are looking for, at least at some level.

Jessica makes a final statement and heartbreaking summary of what is ultimately happening with these female child victims:

"She is rendered powerless, hopeless, and kept silent."

Jessica just hit us hard with some very descriptive words of a child being trafficked. If I pause for a moment and consider those words, I am both heartbroken and enraged. No human, especially a child, should be without power, hope, or a voice.

While most child victims experience what we have described in this chapter, let's not forget what Rachel Thomas taught us regarding the possible recruitment strategy of a fraudulent modeling agency. Additionally, we have not talked about those who are flat-out aggressively kidnapped and violently beaten into submission. Jessica is on record saying she has personally witnessed kids being kept in dog cages and being waterboarded to break their spirit and force their compliance. Another survivor I know once shared with me some of her personal story. She said that at age 13, her trafficker drove her and her best friend out into the desert. The trafficker pulled out a gun and murdered her best friend right in front of her at point-blank range. The friend had broken some kind of rule, and the trafficker took this opportunity to reassert his dominance and demonstrate his version of consequences. Message received!

While the hyper-aggressive stories of torture, beatings, and physical violence certainly exist, they are the smaller percentage of what is typically happening out there. The majority of child victims fall prey to the insidious strategies of the counterfeit boyfriend scenario commonly known as the "Romeo Pimp." This pimp provides imitation love and false security to someone who doesn't know the difference. And of course, the real threat of violence is not only looming but usually present in various forms.

My biggest takeaway from everything I've learned is that most child victims of sex trafficking are groomed and prepared for this life long before their trafficker ever enters the picture. Their already-lived complex trauma has put them into survival mode, which has set a certain trajectory and has created an opening for those with bad intentions.

We've presented, explained, and examined the core business model of sex trafficking. Who are the buyers? Who are the traffickers? And who are the victims? These three questions make up the essence of this devastating crime. To understand these three concepts and how they relate to one another is to understand the basics of what is happening in child sex trafficking.

Now, let's see if we, as men, can find a better way forward! **The time is coming for you to act.**

Part 3
Conclusions and Solutions

"The only thing necessary for the triumph of evil is for good men to do nothing."

Edmund Burke

8

Looking in the Mirror

I am very aware that as a people, we don't agree often. We are divided on pretty much everything. These divisions exist because of political, social, economic, and cultural stand-points and our respective backgrounds. In some instances, differences in opinion can lead to a healthy debate. But when people's lives are on the line, specifically when children are exploited for sexual purposes, we cannot stand divided. We must unite.

On this, we MUST agree. Child sex trafficking CANNOT CONTINUE TO HAPPEN!

The question then becomes, how do we stop it?

Some say that we will never put an end to sexual exploi-tation, that the problem is too big and lucrative to ever be stopped. As for me, I cannot ascribe to that belief. I will not wave the white flag and surrender on this because the stakes are so high—too high! I truly believe that if we band together, we can end the exploitation of children. Tomorrow is too late for the kids who are being abused today, even as you read this book. We can, and we must, dedicate ourselves to the solution of ending human trafficking. There are real solutions out there. I will not give up in this pursuit, and I urge you to join me.

Let's dive into some of the possible solutions that could play a key role in ending human trafficking. This is a complex issue, so I want to be careful not to oversimplify. However, we must engage in a real conversation about a long-lasting, permanent solution. In my humble opinion, there are several varied actions we can take that can conceivably put an end to human trafficking. Consider the following ideas as conversation starters. I have placed these ideas into three categories: Level One: Micro, Level Two: Macro, and Level Three: The Ultimate Solution.

NOTE: Please see Appendix D: Things You Can Do Today! for an extended list of ideas and practical action items in which you can immediately engage. Additionally, see Appendix E: Things Your Church Can Do for a section for our faith-based crowd that can be and needs to be a significant part of the solution.

Alan's Road Map to Abolishing Sex Trafficking
<u>**Level One: Micro**</u>
Look in the Mirror
All of life's issues start with us first. In order to solve a big problem, we must first take an honest look at our place in the problem and work outward from there. We must first look in the mirror! If we are to see the end of trafficking, we each need to make sure that our personal lives are in alignment with ending trafficking. Ending sex trafficking can only be the sum total of all the parts. We need enough men to step up, rise up, and live differently in order to make any real, impactful difference. Below are a few ideas to consider.

Honor, Serve, and Protect Women as a Way of Life
The necessity to start here speaks volumes regarding the root of the problem. The headlines recently have demonstrated anything but honoring, serving, and protecting women. The dark rabbit hole of sex trafficking is the result of a society that has continued to objectify and commodify women. We men must think and act differently toward these important members of humanity. This starts with us as individuals. All the laws and policies we enact won't help one bit if men, one by one, fail to honor, serve, and protect women.

Unfortunately, this calls for a massive paradigm shift for our society. This cannot be relegated to an event, but rather one of the basic principles of life to be lived out daily. There is so much more to say here, but a good starting place is to begin to view women as equals and as people rather than objects. And then challenge the other men around you to do the same. Let this paradigm be reflected in the kind of websites you visit, the kind of music you listen to, the kind of jokes you tell, and the kind of lessons you teach your sons.

Find a Young Boy Without a Father and Become His Mentor
Human trafficking is primarily a male-driven crime. Both the buyers and sellers are predominantly men. How did we get to a place where this is even possible? Simply put, millions of young boys are growing up without a father in a society that largely does not honor women. Many dads are either physically or emotionally absent. The result is a generational wound causing a sickness that is being passed down from broken men to their sons, one after the other. Cyclical dysfunction breeds dysfunction and hurt people *hurt* people. This is especially true for young men.

Our young boys are being groomed by hideous and degrading lyrics from some of the most successful musical artists in our country. They are taking their cues on masculinity from the misogynistic portrayal of men in the movies. The vacuum of healthy male leadership in the lives of so many boys has created a void too easily filled with destructive and exploitive behavior. Find a fatherless boy and invest your time in mentoring him. Society desperately needs an injection of healthy men into the lives of fatherless boys. This is a major commitment, I know. It also might be the single most strategic and effective remedy we have at our disposal.

Be a Leader in Your Community of Men

Stay on the right side of all actions and humor concerning women. How many times have we unknowingly been complicit in sexual abuse and exploitation? How many jokes have we told or laughed at that denigrated women? Have you ever gone with the boys to a strip club? Viewed or paid for sexual exploitation in some way? If we are going to look in the mirror, we need to stand up and be leaders in this area. Put an end to inappropriate conversations and actions demeaning women. Suggest alternative activities that you and your buddies can do. Change the part of the world that you live in. If we get enough men doing this, we'll eventually see impactful change on a large scale.

When my son was in elementary school, there were many days that I would drop him off in the mornings. And every time I did, without fail, I would say the same thing: "Love you, buddy, have a great day. And make sure to be a leader today, not a mindless follower!" We have far too many mindless followers of popular culture and far too much peer pressure these days. We have far too many mindless followers and indulgers in the over-sexualized culture we live in. Most men have not directly created this exploitive and harmful culture; however, most men have participated in it in some way, shape, or form. Men, it's time to step up and be the strong leaders you hope your daughter will one day find and marry. Be countercultural!

Stop Looking at Pornography!

How many men who are looking at pornography are aware that many of the women in the videos are experiencing a form of trafficking? I wonder how many men know that pornography has similar addictive characteristics as hard drugs and can be life-altering. Pornography is a gateway to harder sexual abuse and is a primary grooming mechanism for future sex buyers. As with any addiction, it requires more and more to achieve the same high. In the case of pornography, "more" usually means younger and more violent sites.

How big of a problem is pornography in today's over-sexualized culture? I recently spoke at a private Christian college on the topic of sex trafficking, and a Q and A session afterward veered into this subject matter. I asked a young man how many male students on his campus did he estimate were regularly consuming porn. His answer was "Ninety-eight percent." Couple that with studies that show the average age of first exposure is a tender eight years old, and our future as a society could be in question.

Nicholas Kristof, in his December 4th, 2020 opinion column appearing in *The New York Times,* states that:

> [T]he pornography website known as Pornhub has 3.5 BILLION visits per month, more than Netflix, Yahoo or Amazon." Porn is big business for sure. He points out

that "Pornhub rakes in money from 3 billion ad impressions a day." But what is the essence of this successful business? He states, "Yet there's another side of the company: Its site is infested with rape videos. It monetizes child rapes, revenge pornography, spy cam videos of women showering, racist and misogynist content, and footage of women being asphyxiated in plastic bags.[17]

Benjamin Nolot, founder and CEO of Exodus Cry and executive producer of the documentary *Beyond Fantasy,* explains it this way:

Does the picture on-screen tell the full story? Untold numbers of beautiful women engaged in alluring sexual encounters. It's enticing. I get it. These images prey on our appetite and thirst for intimacy, connection, beauty, and erotic thrill.
I learned something this year, though that shook me.
Most, not some, MOST pornography is created through the use of coercive manipulation. The typical situation involves a girl being told she is going to perform a vanilla sex scene, getting her to sign a consent form, then halfway through the scene, changing the script. In scenarios like this, girls are told they won't be paid unless they complete the scene. Then they are forced to endure the most abusive, degrading, and humiliating sexual acts imaginable. That is called abuse. It was such a wake-up call to realize that most of what is being consumed in porn is not erotic sexual

encounters between two consenting adults but rather the sexual assaults of vulnerable women who have been taken advantage of.

In pornography, sex is cast as a vehicle for the destruction of women, for the pleasure of men. Plain and simple.

We know that sex trafficking victims often report that pornography was filmed of them while they were being trafficked. In an article entitled "How Porn Fuels Sex Trafficking," published August 23rd, 2017, on www.fightthenewdrug.org, a sex trafficking survivor makes a chilling revelation:

"Every time someone watches that film, they are watching me being raped."[18]

The consumption of pornography is not only facilitating the sexual abuse of millions of adults, the pornography industry is attacking the very soul of our humanity while it preys on the absurdly young. During an interview in the documentary *Sex + Money*, Julie Cordua, the CEO and executive director of Thorn, said this:

Child pornography is, in actuality, the documentation of child abuse. We call it child abuse imagery. Seventy-five percent of all the content is actually of prepubescent children and ten percent of these are of infants and toddlers. The volume of the content is so great that it makes it available for people who may otherwise not have participated in it.[19]

If the above statements don't get your attention, I don't know what will! If you are consuming any level of pornography, you are feeding the entire beast and ultimately encouraging sex trafficking with your actions. If you are someone battling the tension of pornography in your personal life, I hope the above statements ruin your appetite. The porn industry is a multi-billion-dollar industry and is absolutely feeding the inhumane scourge of sex trafficking. And in many cases, it literally IS sex trafficking. The problem is that with so many of the porn actors being coerced, in fact, being trafficked into filming, the consumer has no way of distinguishing between who is consenting and who is not.

The porn industry has normalized sexual abuse and exploitation, creating the demand for something more. My advice to those casually consuming pornography is to turn off your computer and get back into bed with your wife. If this seems too difficult to do, I strongly suggest that you get some help before your life crashes into a brick wall. Sex addiction is a real and present danger. If you are currently on the losing end of this battle, you are on the precipice of self-destruction as you participate in the destruction of others. Is that really what you want? Is that who you want to be? You are better than that, and you were meant to do so much more than be shackled by this addiction. There are resources out there to help you. Get the help you need. If this is you, I suggest you start your journey today by going www.fightthenewdrug.org. And then confess your struggle with a friend as you bring this tension into the light. In the light, you can find healing. In the shadows, you find despair. See Appendix F: Resources for Pornography Addiction for suggestions to help you win this battle.

Level Two: Macro

Now that we have paused long enough to examine our personal lives, let's take a look at the bigger picture of society for some possible opportunities to enact positive change. I have included ten ideas to help get our society going in the right direction.

Idea ONE: Acknowledge

First and foremost, as a society, we must acknowledge that sex trafficking is actually happening. I have found that there is a fine line between not knowing what is happening and not *wanting* to know. This is an incredibly challenging topic to discuss. What elected official has the courage to admit that children in their jurisdiction are in danger of being captured, bought, and sold for sex? Or that children from another location are being trafficked and abusively exploited for profit within their boundaries? It would not be good for business, and at the very least, it would not result in reelection. To be fair, there are a brave few in leadership who are meeting this problem head-on. To those rare heroes, we say, "Thank you."

As for the everyday, average citizens, we are shocked to hear of this issue and can only stomach so much conversation about it. In a recent text thread with my old buddies from high school, I texted, "I could tell you guys things that would make your stomach turn." To which one of the 11 buddies on the thread replied, "I'll pass, Alan." My immediate thought was that's exactly why the crime of child sex trafficking has escalated to a multi-billion-dollar industry. People don't have the courage or the stomach to look at it. It's too uncomfortable and much easier to look away. It's nearly impossible to fix something that we can't or won't even talk about, let alone admit is happening in our country.

Idea TWO: Prioritize

After we acknowledge that this is happening, as a society, we must prioritize enough resources to end it. We must make a conscious decision to end it before we have any actual chance of ending it. As a multi-billion-dollar enterprise, ending the tragedy of sex trafficking will be met with great resistance and opposition. Sadly, there are people in powerful positions who are more involved in this crime than we'd care to admit. As men, we must assert leadership where we have influence and prioritize enough resources to get the job done. We'll need to allocate sufficient funding for enhanced forms of law enforcement, mobilize human resources to focus on possible remedies, and direct our government officials to make human trafficking a bigger priority. In a concerted effort, we can do whatever we put our minds to.

Idea THREE: Escalate Penalties for Buyers

We must work and lobby to create more severe penalties for those who buy sex. The current penalty is simply not a grave enough deterrent to dissuade most buyers. There is an urgent need to have thoughtful and effective discussions with lawmakers. The imperative objective would be to create and widely publicize harsh penalties with zero tolerance for those who solicit and/or purchase sex. While this would not eliminate all buyers, it would significantly decrease the number of these sex-related offenses. When the painful consequences and the likelihood of getting caught dramatically outweigh the pleasure of participation, the number of buyers will decrease.

As the demand decreases, the market will shrink along with it. What would be an excruciating penalty that would result in deterrence? Let's dream some up!

Idea FOUR: Escalate Penalties for Exploiters
We must create more severe penalties for those who exploit women and children to sell sex. This is an extension of the point in Idea THREE. While it will not eradicate all exploiters, it would have an effective impact on diminishing the number of young men considering this crime. Several of the pimps who perpetuate these crimes continue to do so with little to no fear of arrest and conviction. They are brazened and boastful regarding the crimes they continue to commit in the name of profit.

I was once shown the public social media profile of a young trafficker. I viewed photo after photo of him showing off handfuls of money and guns while referring to his victims as "his Hoes." My blood began to boil, and at the same time, my heart began to break for what his life had become. He appeared to not have a care in the world as he went about his "business." I won't rest until our society is willing to allocate enough resources to track down every single one of these guys and bring them all to a level of justice that locks them away for a long time. Equally important is a plan to make every effort to rehabilitate their behavior. If one human being is selling another human being—especially teens and children for sex—they should never be able to engage in this destructive practice ever again. If we eliminate sex traffickers, then sex trafficking disappears.

*It is noteworthy to point out that there are growing numbers of female traffickers as well as a growing number of male victims. There are likely more of each than we can account for because this egregious crime is driven by financial profit. Money does not discriminate, and it has no master.

Idea FIVE: Create Opportunities

At the same time we are pursuing and arresting traffickers, we must also focus on creating better education and employment opportunities for young inner-city males. As we learned from the former trafficker I had coffee with, he was trying to survive while growing up in extremely adverse circumstances. He was exposed to very few viable options in an environment where very few positive options were ever modeled. For us to be singularly focused on existing traffickers while neglecting to divert them at a young age would be akin to parking an ambulance down below a cliff rather than building a fence near the edge.

Idea SIX: Employ Technological Resources

We need enough resources for technology that enables us to track and prosecute Internet predators. Great strides are being made in this area. However, the Internet is a vast world of information and commerce. We need all the brilliant minds who were intelligent enough to create and improve the World Wide Web to now develop ways to safeguard it against online exploitation for profit. The FBI recently estimated that there are upward of 900,000 predators online. It's been said that the smartphone has more technology than it took to place a man on the moon, yet it has become the twenty-first-century brothel. I am confident that there are currently geniuses in the industry who are creating online tracking tools. However, it is imperative that we combine high technology with new regulatory laws that will have a profound impact on what is legal to do on the Internet.

Idea SEVEN: Monitor Technology

This one relies heavily on the previous point. There must be a priority to allocate enough resources to track down and close all apps and websites used for human trafficking and exploitation, with an emphasis on those involving minors. We should not be living in a world where you can go onto a website or a social app and order a child to have sex with. There is not a more direct and emphatic way to state this! Nor should one be able to view child pornography. This is a nonnegotiable, zero-tolerance proposition. The goal is an unrelenting effort to shut them all down and prosecute everyone who is involved in the creation of these sites. Naturally, there is a reaction to wave the banner of "free speech" or invoke some other legal loophole. I am certain that competent, educated individuals in Washington can figure out an appropriate legislative remedy if they felt pressure from the voters they have sworn to represent and serve.

The 2018 FOSTA/SESTA legislation (House bill "Fight Online Sex Trafficking Act," and Senate bill "Stop Enabling Sex Traffickers Act") signed into law in 2018 was a giant step in the right direction. It immediately provided the legal tools necessary to prosecute those selling children online. The notorious Backpage.com was closed overnight and their CEO was arrested, which was a huge step in the right direction. However, considering the amount of money involved, there is no doubt that those working their way around this legislation and seeking other alternatives will resurface. Shutting down Backpage. com was a crippling blow, but kids are still being sold online elsewhere, including popular social media platforms. We must be vigilant and relentless on this one. The Internet is a major player in this crime.

Idea EIGHT: Educate the Vulnerable
We need to create and deliver educational and awareness curriculum on a large scale and make it available in places where the most vulnerable kids are located. Too many young kids have inadequate knowledge, awareness, or education surrounding the predatory nature of this victimization. As a result, they are left vulnerable and susceptible to exploitation without even knowing what they are stepping into. Let's prevent this crime from ever happening, in as many places as possible, through early warning and educating those who are most vulnerable. Basic knowledge and awareness are integral to preventing and stopping a crime before it ever starts.

Idea NINE: Do Not Decriminalize Prostitution
Make it a priority to never legalize prostitution.* There is a percentage of the population who believe that full decriminalization of prostitution would somehow be a helpful and productive measure. Among them are some influential elected politicians who are seeking to push this dangerous ideal. The argument persists that it would somehow provide legal protections for "sex workers," which they believe would be beneficial for them. The whole point of the solution to this crime is to eliminate the marketplace, not facilitate it. Basic Business 101 dictates that when a market expands and the demand expands, the available product must also increase in order to meet that demand. Our goal is not only to decrease sex trafficking but to abolish it—COMPLETELY!

The full decriminalization of prostitution will undoubtedly expand the market demand for sex workers. This will result in vulnerable minors being targeted as new "product" in order to meet the needs of the expanding marketplace. It is important to note that the majority of adult sex workers began when they were NOT of legal, consenting age. They were generally forced into it as a minor, having no knowledge of the fact that a felony was being committed against them. The full decriminalization of prostitution would be the final slap in the face from society to the countless victims being enslaved to sex trafficking. It would send a hopeless message to victims if we were to legally turn our backs on them and openly allow their abuse not only to continue but intensify.

I had a discussion on social media with a few people on this very topic. One of the guys, young and arrogant, actually called me a moron for defending my stance that legalizing prostitution would effectively hurt more people than it would help. Perhaps I don't have all the answers, but I personally know people who do.

Rebecca Bender, sex-trafficking survivor and founder of the Rebecca Bender Initiative and author of *In Pursuit of Love,* co-authored a very poignant letter. Her letter with the heading "Survivors of prostitution and sex trafficking" was circulated, and signatures were gathered from members of various communities. The letter was entitled "An Open Letter to All Presidential Candidates." Contained in this letter, written and signed by those with actual lived experience, was the following:

"Decriminalizing the sex trade in its entirety would have disastrous consequences. Do not be confused—full decriminalization means allowing pimps, sex buyers, and brothel owners to operate with impunity. Sex trafficking (including that of children) and organized crime increases when pimping and sex buying are legalized."

Does it really sound appropriate to legalize the buying and selling of vulnerable people, many of whom are minors? Read that again and say it out loud. "The legalization of the buying and selling of vulnerable people." We would be wise to always pay close attention to those with actual lived experience. The vast majority of survivors of prostitution and trafficking want to put an end to the buying and selling of vulnerable people, and know firsthand that the best way to do so is to ensure that pimping and sex buying remain behaviors that aren't encouraged or tolerated.

*Prostitution is a commonly understood legal term. Those actively working toward the eradication of trafficking refrain from using this word as it is a derogatory label that suggests "choice." Rarely do these women have a real choice, and as minors, they absolutely have no choice at all. I only use it here because there is a legal conversation happening in our society around this term, and it provides a common understanding.

Idea TEN: Public Office

Commit to vote people into positions of power who agree with and will actively make all the above a real priority. Let's make this a litmus test for election into public office, at every level. We must send a message to our political candidates to include all of the above in their party platform. If they fail to clearly communicate their opposition and strategic action to execute on these ideas during campaign speeches, debates, and media messaging, then they don't get our vote. We must make this critical issue a condition of employment for our elected officials at local, state, and national levels.

Level Three: The Ultimate Solution

I realize that it's a very bold statement to claim that I know what the ultimate solution is. However, humbly speaking, it's true. I believe I do know what the ultimate solution is. The ultimate solution will not be found in a new law or policy, as important as those things are. The ultimate solution is a matter of the heart, and that's what makes it tricky. It is deeply personal to every man.

This may be obvious by now, but let me be clear. Although there are plenty of women involved in all facets of human trafficking, Men are the biggest part of the problem! Who creates and consumes most of the pornography? MEN. Who visits most of the strip clubs and illicit massage parlors? MEN. Who are the chief exploiters of women? MEN. Who represents the majority of the buyers of sex? MEN. And finally, of the two parents who bring a child into this world, which parent is most likely to be absent? MEN.

This is on us, guys. The world has never been sicker and unhealthier than it is right now. We are complicit in leading it down this dark and painful path. WE are complicit in this abuse due to apathy and inaction at best and by willing participation at worst.

Now for some good news. If we have pinpointed the problem, it means that we can determine a solution. We see this in medicine all the time. If a cancerous growth exists, often it can be cut out. I have personally had that done twice on my shoulder. If you break a bone, it can be x-rayed and placed in a cast.

When you can pinpoint a particular problem area, there is a favorable chance of administering a successful treatment. In this case, men are undoubtedly the problem. Therefore, if we know men are the problem, then it stands to reason that men are also the solution. Great! We're 50 percent there!

Simply intervening with preventative education, more substantial penalties, and better technology will certainly inhibit some of this behavior. But my fear is that the die has already been cast for far too many men. In many cases, they have grown up in an environment that lacks options, guidance, accountability, and opportunity. Far too many boys have grown up without a healthy father figure. Many are left to navigate a tough road, feeling alone as they attempt to figure out who they are and what purpose they serve in this world. Moms are critical to their development, but a present and engaged dad makes all the difference for a little boy.

Are You Ready for It?
Here it is ... FINALLY, my ultimate solution for sex trafficking in which we can all play a part. In fact, for it to work, each of us MUST play a part. It is the ultimate solution to not only ending human trafficking but many of the other ills in this world as well. This is crystal clear to me; simple in concept but admittedly difficult and lengthy in execution.

Ultimate Solution Phase One
First, be the right kind of man. Be the man who honors, serves, and protects women. Start in your own home. Let your dating or marriage relationship become the gold standard for what it means to love and serve well. Make this a priority. Live it out loud for all to see, especially your children. Your daughters

desperately need to see what is possible and how they should expect to be treated by men. Teach them to accept nothing less. Too many little girls grow up influenced by social media, pop music, and all manner of destructive messaging. Your daughter is watching, and she needs a solid example of a strong, healthy man to measure all others against. Do this, and she will be better for it.

Your sons desperately need to see a picture of how a healthy, authentic man should live. He needs to see healthy masculinity that honors, serves, protects, and sacrifices. You can start doing this right now—today! Make a statement with your life in this regard. Your family and your community are watching and learning from you. What are you teaching them?

Ultimate Solution Phase Two

Raise your sons to honor, serve, and protect women. Expect nothing less. Zero tolerance. Model it, teach it, expect it. Monitor websites viewed and music listened to. Lovingly correct him when he fails and celebrate his victories when he succeeds. Remain in constant dialogue over pertinent topics. This is not an event to be had with your son—it's a lifestyle to be lived, experienced, and consistently observed over many years.

Far too many young boys are growing up thinking that dishonoring and exploiting women is not only common behavior but that it's expected. Start with YOU and your home. Raise your sons to be countercultural. *Inspect* what you *expect* and reward the right behaviors when you see them. When my son was in junior high and was starting to explore the Internet, we did a few things. First, we let it be known what type of websites were banned in our home. To make sure he was compliant, we installed a tracking software that e-mailed us every site visited and every keystroke made from our computer. In fact, one time I busted one of his friends during a sleepover for inappropriately communicating with someone from our computer. You should have seen his face when I asked him about it. We also banned any song that was marked "Explicit." I knew that a song marked "explicit" usually meant degrading sex and demeaning women in some way. If one "accidentally" showed up on his account, I quickly deleted it or smashed the CD right in front of him. Inspect what you expect!

You know that smartphone you gave to your son (or will give to him)? On day one, let him know that it is, in fact, YOUR phone that you are lending him. It's not his phone at all. And because of that, you have the right to take it and inspect it anytime you like. If you are paying for his phone service, it is YOUR phone, and therefore you have all rights to it. There are so many ugly apps out there promoting brutal behavior that will find their way onto your son's phone if you don't keep a close eye on it. There are so many ugly lyrics and images out there that can find their way onto your son's phone if you are not paying attention. Make it a regular practice to inspect *YOUR* phone that you were nice enough to let him borrow. Raise your kids from an early age to say NO to certain conversations and actions and set them up to be strong, positive leaders throughout their adolescence. So many destructive habits are formed simply because we have either been asleep at the wheel or failed to see the gravity of them.

Can we make the commitment to enact Levels One and Two above and also invest in the next generation of males by providing them with strong, healthy role models who intentionally respect and honor women? If we stack hands on this, we may actually have a shot at ending the abuse of women and delivering a death blow to sex trafficking. I can imagine what some of you are thinking: All of this seems like it would make a positive difference, but over the long haul, it seems like a long-term investment that could take quite a while to implement and even longer to see significant benefits, if ever. Yes, you are correct. That's why there is no time to waste. We need to get started, like yesterday.

Additionally, refer to Appendix D: Things You Can Do Today! for a list of easily accessible and practical things that you can do right now ... TODAY! There is plenty of low-hanging fruit regarding things we can do quickly and easily. However, we cannot make a meaningful and sustainable difference if we are unwilling to make the important life changes that will impact tomorrow on a much grander scale. If we can motivate and inspire enough men to get after it and own these directives, we may actually have a real shot. I believe that! Do YOU?

In Conclusion

In the words of Colonel Nathan Jessup, aka Jack Nicholson in *A Few Good Men*, in one of the greatest courtroom movie scenes of all time, he says:

"I have a greater responsibility than you can possibly fathom."[20]

Colonel Jessup was very clear, although maybe a bit misguided in his approach. This is our responsibility, men. It's on us. We created this mess and have passively allowed it to run rampantly out of control. Now it's up to us to step up and end this egregious dehumanization. Step into your God-given responsibility to honor, serve, and protect women. Start small in your own life and do whatever you can to help that paradigm grow and shift—one man at a time, one community at a time. If we commit ourselves to affecting real change, we can see this end. The question is, will we own our responsibility, our part, in this? We established earlier that *the ultimate solution is a matter of the heart.* It is a heart issue, and the convictions of our hearts must urge us to act! It starts right here, right now, with YOU and with me.

It's Go Time!

"I firmly believe that any man's finest hour, the greatest fulfilment of all that he holds dear, is that moment when he has worked his heart out for a good cause and lies exhausted on the field of battle—victorious."

Vince Lombardi

"A life is not important except in the impact it has on other lives."

Jackie Robinson

9

Profiles in Authentic Masculinity

As we consider new ways to think and act, sometimes the best path forward is studying people who are already successful in your area of interest. Let's see if we can learn a thing or two from those already doing it!

I want to challenge your thinking by inviting you to take a glimpse into the lives of a few of my friends. The goal of this whole conversation is much bigger than the eradication of human trafficking. Rather, it is to help inspire a generation of men to live stronger and more positively impactful lives that exemplify the healthiest possible version of masculinity. If we can accomplish this on a grand scale, the plight of human trafficking will most certainly diminish and, at best, disappear altogether. If we can get enough men living the right way, we'll cure a host of other destructive issues as well.

I believe the following men to be honorable husbands, great fathers, and strong men. Are they all perfect? NO. Made mistakes? Of course! Are they strong, active males committed to doing the very best that they can to make a difference? YES, they are! My hope is that you will find some common themes that will resonate with you and perhaps integrate them into your own life and/or personal philosophy.

You're about to discover a gold mine of insights and information. Be prepared to take some notes as I proudly introduce you to some of my friends who will attempt to define "Authentic Masculinity."

Ben Chambers

Formerly in the entertainment industry, currently developing and mentoring college students, lover of football, and always a husband and father of four

It is my personal belief and philosophy that "authentic masculinity" can be found in that which is countercultural to the common idea of masculinity. Being authentic essentially means being REAL. Masculinity is the *healthy* expression of being a man with regard to your thoughts, words, deeds, and actions. A man with unhealthy masculinity allows cultural norms, false expectations, and other men to dictate his actions and reactions to any given situation. As a man, I have one true power—the power to *choose* how I act and react. Authentic masculinity dictates that I take personal responsibility for the fact that my choices will have *communal* or socially impactful consequences that can strengthen or destroy both myself and others. At the heart of authentic masculinity is the power to make the *right* choices in relation to any given situation that results in beneficial, impactful change and/or growth in one's self and society at large—World-changers.

I believe that Jesus was the most countercultural man to walk the earth. He also embodied authentic masculinity—the kind that inspires me to *choose* humility in victory and grace in defeat. Likewise, I can choose the integrity of what is right over what is easy. I can choose to think about the possible consequences of my actions before I act and let that be my guide. I can choose to take responsibility and learn from failure because it helps me to extend grace and encourage others who fail. I can choose to see the value of others based upon their humanness and not their social/cultural status or lack thereof. I can choose to stand up for and even protect the underdog or the weak because arrogance, bullying, exploitation, and manipulation are sure signs of weakness and insecurity. I can choose to see another man as a threat, an opponent, or a challenger. Or, I can choose to see him as a potential friend or brother in need of encouragement, guidance, and direction. I can choose to seek peace first, but be prepared to protect and defend when necessary. I can choose to see a woman's body solely as an object of desire or see her humanness as a person of value—a daughter, sister, mother, or wife.

It is authentically masculine to be better at giving than at taking, yet remaining humble enough to receive. It's knowing that the goodness of laughing is equal to the healthiness of crying because real emotion is authenticity. The point is simple. I, Ben Chambers, get to choose what the authenticity of my masculinity looks like. I do not have to allow society, media, culture, my ego, or popularity dictate what that looks like. Finally, the ultimate goal of the authentically masculine is to be the man that people can trust and rely on, the husband that your wife misses during her day, the man that your son would aspire to be, and the man that you would want your daughter to marry.

Ryan Dalton

*Former Special Agent in the US Department of State,
husband, and father*

Authentic masculinity is a hard concept to define. Just when you think you've nailed down a good working definition, someone comes along and defies it. I've learned authentic masculinity isn't about your hobbies, how you dress, who your friends are, how much money you make, or how much you can bench press. Authentic masculinity is rooted in strong character, and a part of strong character is treating people as an end unto themselves rather than a means to something you want for yourself.

You will never look into the eyes of a person who does not possess value and dignity that must be honored. The man who buys sex ignores this timeless truth and uses a victim as merely a means to fulfill his distorted sexuality, effectively using that person as a tool for masturbation, and removes the human connection, which should be born from genuine intimacy. Compare this to the man who treats all people with the dignity they deserve, and in his daily decisions and behaviors, elevates those around him toward goodness and toward the best version of themselves. This man is living out a central component of authentic masculinity.

This is not to say authentic masculinity does not involve struggle. In the heart of every man is duality—there is a quiet, internal war between a hedonist and a saint. The hedonist screams "me!" and the saint whispers "them." The daily relational choices we make define our trajectory toward or away from authentic masculinity. How we treat those around us, especially when no one is watching, reveals our character. It's never too late to become the man you want to become.

Kellan Lutz

Film and television actor (Twilight, Hercules, Expendables, etc.), father, husband, entrepreneur

I've been lucky enough to get some really cool roles so far in my acting career. Some fictional, some real people, but a lot of them have been playing the role of the "hero." I think it's shifting now, but from really the beginning of time when a "hero" or, better yet, a "superhero" was mentioned, you likely thought of a man who was strong, well built, and did something great for those weaker than themselves in some capacity. They were tough, not driven by emotion, and proud. Now, none of those are negative qualities. In fact, I think those are some of the qualities God created man to have and operate in. But somewhere along the line, those qualities were perverted and twisted, and a major portion of society equated masculinity or "being a man" with making sure everyone knew they were tough, not only showing zero emotion, but it was deemed weak to even be aware of your internal emotional state, and you have to have a huge ego that people pick up on as soon as you enter any room. As a result, we have a large group of men who lack compassion, empathy, and emotional awareness and are walking around actually abusing others, thinking that is what masculinity is. But most can see and agree that those who try to act the toughest and the most confident are actually incredibly insecure, attempting to control everything and everyone around them to prove and reinforce this idea of masculinity that they learned somewhere along the way. I couldn't clearly articulate what being a man was, but I knew I didn't want to be that kind of man.

As I was praying about how I would define "Authentic Masculinity" and what it means to "be a man," I was struck with how different I would define that now versus when I was younger. As a kid, like most young guys, I had an idea of what it was to "be a man" based on what I had seen. Being a man meant going to work, being the provider, being the head of the household, and ... that's about it. But as I grew and got closer and closer to God, He started to show me what it truly was to be a man through who He is and how He created man.

It says in the Bible in Genesis 1:27 that God created man in His own image. It also says in John 1:4 that God IS Love. So, being the math-brained guy I am, if A=B and B=C, then A=C. Man was created in the image of love. But what is it to reflect love in such a way that you embody it? We throw around the term "love" often, and as a result, it truly has lost its weight and has become far less sacred than it was designed to be. I think we've all been guilty of a statement like, "I love pizza!" But do you really "love" pizza, or just really like it? As I went deeper with God about what love truly is, He brought me to a passage in Corinthians that I've heard more times than I can count and has been recited at countless weddings. Heck, even at my wedding! But 1 Corinthians 13:4-7 says this:

Love is patient, love is kind. It does not envy, it does not boast, it is not proud.

It does not dishonor others, it is not self-seeking, it is not easily angered, it keeps no record of wrongs. Love does not delight in evil but rejoices with the truth. It always protects, always trusts, always hopes, always perseveres.

So, if that is what love is, and God is love, and man is created in His image, I have come to this conclusion about what truly being a man is:

A man should be patient. He should be kind. He shouldn't envy, or boast, or be prideful. A man doesn't dishonor others. He doesn't seek to put himself first. He isn't easily angered and doesn't keep a record of wrongs. He doesn't delight in evil but rejoices with the truth. A man always protects, always trusts, always perseveres.

Obviously, this is a tall order, and no man, let alone any human on the planet other than Jesus himself, can live up to that. However, without vision and clear purpose and without aiming at a mark in life, you will get distracted and caught up in places you never meant to go. I've seen it countless times in my industry where people come with a dream but not a vision and end up getting swallowed up in a city and an industry that's literally designed to chew you up and spit you out. Rather than looking at 1 Corinthians as a destination that I have to get to in order to be a "real man," I look at it as a roadmap to a destination that I'll be striving toward until the day I die. I know I will never embody every single thing perfectly because I am not perfect, but by inviting God who IS love on my journey to try to embody everything Corinthians says love is, how much better of a man will I be by the end of my time on earth?

Detective Ray Bercini

*30-year career in the LA County Sheriff's
Department, former Gang Intervention Unit Leader
in the LA County Human Trafficking Task Force,
husband, father, and grandfather*

Growing up as a young boy and remembering my experiences of those early years brought to mind the vivid images of being abandoned by my father and disappointed by many of the males who should have been my heroes and mentors. I was mostly raised by my mother, grandmother, and aunts. Although I have such great respect for all the women in my life, I still felt I was deprived of the opportunity to have healthy relationships with any male role models who could have taught me and guided me well.

Over the years, I have searched for the male relationships that I felt could validate me as a capable and worthy man. I longed to be proven, and I attempted to impress anyone from my gender that I was the toughest kid around. Even back then, I could feel in my soul that the way I would act out was not who I really was as a person. Everything I did was a performance, and at times I didn't think I could keep up the act. Through my journey, I joined the ranks of law enforcement, which helped me stay in control of my machismo persona, but this would also become a daily struggle. Please understand, I'm not saying that these moments and situations are inherently wrong— I have learned so much from my experiences. I love and embrace my masculinity. However, through much growth and maturity, I came to a crossroad and a deep realization that I needed to be more authentic in my masculinity. You see, being groomed and conditioned by the environment that I grew up in and groups I was influenced by strongly shaped the man I became. So, it is also very important to me to acknowledge the positive influential males I've befriended throughout my lifetime. I was fortunate enough to surround myself with positive role models and capture the essence and strength of all those individuals. It had a huge impact on my ability to live and thrive as a good friend, brother, father, and now grandfather.

Unfortunately, it's not the case for many. I believe a significant part of our society has suffered from a loss of the authentic father figure. We see many fatherless boys and young men acting out bad behavior in ways that shocks us to our core, and we struggle to make sense of what's happening. While they are starving for the praise and acceptance of a loving father, their disappointment has fueled resentment, bitterness, and ultimately, hatred. Although disheartening, this vulnerability allows for an opportunity with both positive and negative influences.

I've personally committed my heart to be an authentic changemaker and become a positive male role model to the fatherless. Witnessing so many men desperately living for the praise and acceptance of others in a dire attempt to fulfill an immediate and egocentric gratification has proved exhausting. It cannot and will not ever satisfy the soul. I've learned that to be truly authentic, it first had to start with me. I needed to start the process of becoming whole. To be whole required that I balanced out my life, spiritually, mentally, physically, and emotionally. Once becoming more balanced, I experienced a transformation and started feeling whole. This brought on an inner peace and joy and gave me a renewed confidence. I realized that my transformation of becoming more complete within would ultimately work its way out and reflect the authentic person I was purposed to be. This is a choice, a belief, and my mission is to speak and influence as many young men as will listen.

No other challenge in my life was greater than raising my children. I believe as a father, there is no better test to your authenticity than being exposed and vulnerable to your kids. I valued them more than anything in my life. I wanted them to feel safe, secure, and proud of their big, strong dad. Over the years, I tried to share everything I could with them because I wanted to instill and model the values that I held as worthy in my own life. Please know that I was not perfect, and they will all attest to that. My three daughters are all grown now and married. Nothing makes me prouder than to see the men they chose to spend their lives with. I would like to say they chose men like their dad, but in my opinion, they all chose men who are better than their dad. All of my sons-in-law are amazing people, and they have proven to be real, loving, and authentic human beings. I am still raising my son, and the future holds great promise for him. He is a kind, loving, and respectful boy, and I have no doubt he will treat others unconditionally with fairness and compassion.

I am a man of faith, and I do draw strength from God. He is my source of love that is unconditional. This is where I have the strength and ability to do acts of kindness and remain compassionate to anyone I may encounter in my lifetime. If I demonstrate authentic love and compassion, I believe others will see it in me, and my actions will be deemed pure of heart. I've always taught my children to look through the eyes of God when they view the world, walk in the Spirit as they travel life's path, and follow the ways of the Lord when they serve others without condition.

Geoff LaTendresse

Former Fire Chief and one of the "Braveheart" dads,
husband, and father of two

As I sit here and write this, eyes filled with tears, I don't feel much like an authentic man. The truth is, I am in the middle of one of the worst storms of my life, and I'm feeling pretty beat up. To make matters worse, I don't feel like I'm living up to the standard of authenticity I've set for myself. I'm a man of deep faith and have steadfastly rooted every aspect of my life in my faith.

It started with my dad passing away last October. I loved my dad. He was the greatest man I've ever known, and we enjoyed a special relationship. All I could do was helplessly watch until he finally took his last breath. I felt like I was an intruder in a sacred moment, and I'm still haunted by it.

The real heartbreak is that I've had a front-row seat to a persistent and now rapid decline in my daughter's mental and physical health as a result of her ongoing battle with anxiety and OCD.

She has been in therapy for several years now, and while she made gains early, she is worse off now than she has ever been. She is a shadow of the bright, joyful, fill-the-room-with-light person that she has always been, and I'm feeling pretty overwhelmed and, truthfully, at the moment, very hopeless.

I don't feel very authentic at this moment. All I feel right now is rocked, and I'm desperately trying not to be wrecked. When I pray, I can only get two or three words out because the weight of all this has compressed my spiritual chest so much that I feel like there's not enough oxygen in my spiritual lungs to get full sentences out.

I suppose this is what someone pursuing authentic masculinity does. He remains steadfast, keeps showing up, and does his best to stay the course regardless of his obstacles. An authentic male leans into heartache rather than runs from it. He might even shed a tear or two (or many) along the way.

Louie Greek

Former military, law enforcement, and undercover operator disrupting trafficking rings and recovering children around the world. Currently with Truckers Against Trafficking

Coming from a career spanning over a combined 30 years in law enforcement and the military, I have experienced all forms of masculinity. There's the toxic masculinity exhibited when men in these career fields make jokes that degrade women or when they cope with residual trauma by purchasing sex. On the other end of the spectrum, there are men in these professions who stand up for victims. They come to the aid of exploited women and children and encourage other men to do the same. The latter is exactly the authentic masculinity that is so desperately needed in our culture today in order to change how men view women and spark that social shift needed to reduce the exploitation of vulnerable people.

I spent six years working undercover in some of the world's largest and most sinister red-light districts. During that time, part of my work involved assisting with the recovery of victims of sex trafficking. I saw firsthand the most toxic examples of masculinity, as men, day in and day out, victimized young girls and boys. I witnessed fathers taking their sons to a brothel to induct them into what they believed was manhood but what is actually a detrimental cycle of dehumanization of their many victims.

Throughout my life and career, I have had good men with positive morals and character encourage authentic masculinity. These men are war heroes, fellow investigators, pastors, and undercover agents. They are men who embody everything it means when we envision masculinity. They are physically strong, mentally tough, and encouraging leaders who hold men accountable for how we conduct ourselves.

It took years to start realizing that some of the things I learned in those alpha male communities came with negatively toxic aspects of masculinity. Like going to strip clubs after boot camp to fit in with new comrades, celebrating the promotion of the new police detective with a lap dance, or sharing porn with your roommates while deployed in a war zone. All of this is toxic, and all of it can lead down a path of dehumanization, victimization, and thus, the demand for commercial sex.

So, when you and your comrades port for the first time after being out to sea (or perhaps on a Friday night after a long week at work), and someone suggests heading to the strip clubs or brothels, my hope is that this new generation of authentic males will be bold in identifying the dangers those locations and activities pose the innocent victims. If more men boldly joined this fight and held other men accountable, we would see a reduction in the demand for commercial sex, fewer victims, and a culture where men can be authentically masculine.

Adam LaRoche

*Former Major League Baseball player, current
deputy, always a husband and a father*

I believe, maybe deep down, that most men go through
life with a fear of being discovered, found out, identified as a
fraud. Why is that? Maybe because we are trying to be someone we are not. The question we need to ask is, "Who am I?"
I'm almost 40 years old, and I don't know that I could give
you a crystal-clear picture of who I am. But I do know that my
view of "what a true man is" has changed significantly over the
years. A younger me would have probably described this man
as having success, strength, and status (to name a few).

Not to brag, but I have achieved all of those, and it didn't
come close to answering those questions. Through most of my
school years, and even on into my major league career, I was
searching for things that I thought would bring happiness and
satisfaction. Whether that be women, drugs, alcohol, money,
etc. We chase and we chase, expecting a different result, and
it doesn't happen. Sure, it might bring temporary satisfaction,
but then what? It's a never-ending cycle of trying to fill that
hole in our hearts that many men have lived their entire lives
trying to figure out but never do.

I got the answers when I began being the man that God
wanted me to be. The greatest example of a "true man" that I
have been able to find is Jesus as a human being. The more
I understand his life, the more I realize he doesn't want us to
be sissies. He wants us to be warriors and has put that into
every man's DNA. This country and our society will say otherwise. They will say we need the fanciest cars and clothes and

the hottest woman to prove we are "a man." It's a lie. Now, don't get me wrong, I like nice things. I love a good whiskey and even an occasional great cigar, but those things don't define who I am. I have found more confidence and clarity in who I am since I began caring more about others than I do myself.

I have seen this for years in our military warriors—specifically, our special operator-type units. These are the manliest of men, and the love and care they have for each other is like nothing I have ever seen. They are asked to go into the darkest areas on earth, for very little money, and fight for those who can't fight for themselves. Now, I'm not saying that we are all called to be Rambo or that all of our soldiers' hearts are in the right place, but what I am saying is we will find more significance in our lives when we can take the mask off, stop trying to be who everyone else wants us to be, and confidently use the strengths that God has given us to be a warrior for others.

I loved playing baseball all those years. It was an incredible platform to reach a lot of people, but the best part about it was that it set the stage for what I get to do now. I get to serve those who have spent their lives serving us by hosting hunting trips for our combat warriors at our ranch in Kansas. In between those events, I get to work with some of the strongest men and women I've ever been around in the fight against sex trafficking.

Dr. Scott Lisea

Campus pastor at Westmont College, husband, and father to three boys

I am considering this question while on another visit to Uganda, a land where the stakes are immediately clear and very high in regard to this issue. Uganda has the highest birth rate on the African continent. It also has a staggering level of fatherlessness. There are currently over three million orphans in Uganda, largely due to a systemic and low understanding of what a real man is. Here, a man is one who "does as he pleases with whom he pleases," spreading his seed with whomever he desires, including his neighbor's wife.

Because the cultural message regarding manhood here is so clearly destructive, it helps me to see how the same is distinctly true in my culture in the US. I grew up largely "fatherless" due to an absentee, alcoholic father. In contrast to the cultural messages in Uganda, as well as the ever-confusing ideas of gender and issues of manhood in our own culture and throughout the world, Scripture reveals to us a radically different picture of manhood. There are several key principles we find in Scripture, but one I wish to highlight here is the concept of strength.

Strength is not defined by any one personality, body type, or set of interests. Rather, it comes from being shaped by God's love in order to love others. Essentially, our strength is something God wants to develop within us, manifesting as character, compassion, and integrity, and he calls us to cooperate and participate with him—to love him with "all our strength."

When a man loves God with all of his will, he is shaped into a person who is free to love others. Simply stated, our strength is not for ourselves. We are strong for others. Our development in strength is to benefit the women and children and the marginalized around us.

When a man does not know who he belongs to, nor has the reassurance that he is securely loved by God, he looks in strange places for his validation. In contrast, when his roots and future are secured, he is free to love and serve. We see this in Jesus' life. At his baptism, he hears the Father's voice tell him, "You are my beloved son in whom I am well pleased." Before he had done a thing, he was loved. Fast forward to John 13, when we see Jesus perform a radical act of service to his disciples by washing their feet. It says he did this because he knew that he came from God and was returning to God. His validation was in place. What did it produce? Service. Our strength is not for ourselves. It is for the women in our lives, the children in our lives, and the vulnerable in our world. We come most alive when we take all of our strength and employ it for their benefit rather than our image, immature versions of masculinity, or self-absorption.

I love adventure, sport, and challenge as much as the next guy. But you know when I'm most alive? When I find places where I can use everything God has given me to raise someone up who needs to be lifted, when my words and actions build security in others, and where my actions and resources make a difference for someone in need.

Bazzel Baz

Founder of The Association for the Recovery of Children (ARC is comprised of former and active intelligence, military, and law enforcement personnel dedicated to the recovery of missing and exploited children, foreign and domestic), Former Captain USMC and CIA officer, author of Something Bigger Than Overthrowing Small Governments

The one term that most accurately defines a real man, an authentic man, is "nobility." Nobility has everything to do with having high character. In my mind, being "noble" equals being trustworthy. People follow trustworthy leaders. Trustworthy leaders will lay their lives down for the innocent, and they will never take advantage of other people.

A noble man is built to serve, not to take. The minute a man takes, he loses all credibility. An authentic man considers these questions: What do I care about? What does God think about me? What do I think about myself?

Manhood is not a boy's club where we cover for each other. It's about holding people accountable. Micah 6:8 gives us our marching orders: "To act justly and to love mercy and to walk humbly with your God."

I've been downrange with real men, and I've seen them in action. Real men stand their watch and guard the gate. They don't let anyone come in and do harm to innocent people. Real men, honorable men, noble men, will rise to the top. Those who don't will be crushed by our feet. Most men who think they are men are not really men at all. There are not many authentic, noble men.

Regarding trafficking: You must care to get involved. In order to care, you must first be aware. Now that you have read this book, you have no excuse. What are you going to do? You've got to put your "big boy pants" on to save kids from trafficking. I am not looking to have every man get involved. The quantity of men is not as important as the quality of men.

Trafficking is not about the word "trafficking," it's about the crime being committed.

Cages, beatings, slavery, auctions. Until there are boots on the ground going after kids, we haven't done anything. Consuming information doesn't help anyone.

Men have allowed themselves to lose their power. The reason we don't have more men involved in anti-trafficking efforts is because they are cowards. Those who have the time but don't get involved are cowards. Real men would stop this in its tracks. They would come alongside all the good men who are already fighting and would help in whatever way they could. We may never be able to totally stop trafficking, but if we had more men involved in this fight, we could put a big dent in it.

Manhood isn't defined by what you do; it is defined by who you are. God created man and set the game plan for us. By his grace, he allows us to be a part of his great plan. The very breath in our lungs belongs to God. As you follow God's plan, you become accountable to him. When we follow our plan, we fail. And quite frankly, when it comes to saving children from trafficking, it is a mission we cannot afford to fail at.

Powerful Statements
There were so many powerful phrases and statements made by my friends above. To summarize, here are a few of them.

Be countercultural.
I have the power to choose.
Personal responsibility.
Trustworthiness and reliability.
Answers came from God.
Strength is shaped by God's love.
Our strength is not for ourselves.
Authentic masculinity is rooted in strong character.
The saint whispers "them."
It's never too late to become the man you want to become.

I needed to start the process of becoming whole.

He remains steadfast, keeps showing up.

Leaders hold men accountable.

Be bold.

Man was created in the image of love.

A real man, an authentic man, is "Nobility."

Trustworthy leaders will lay their lives down for the innocent.

The minute a man takes, he loses all credibility.

Manhood is not a boy's club where we cover for each other.

Now that you have read this book, you have no excuse.

Men have allowed themselves to lose their power.

They are cowards.

Real men would stop this (trafficking) in its tracks.

Manhood isn't defined by what you do, it is defined by who you are.

Special Circumstances:

Before we end this chapter, I want to make a special note to those men who are not currently living with their sons or may have some version of shared custody. Please do everything you can to lay aside the differences you have had with your child's mother and stay engaged with your son at all costs. They need you to be close. They will feed off your example of manhood, whether you are aware of it or not. They need a safe, healthy place to learn and practice what it means to be a man, and the best place to do that is with you.

And for those moms who might be reading this, if your sons' father is not in the picture, I encourage you to find a trusted male you are close to and appropriately invite him into your son's life. You are doing an amazing job, but your boy still needs to experience the healthy influences and input of manhood from an older, trusted male figure. Men and women are different, and your son will benefit greatly from having a balance of both in his life.

"The world is a dangerous place to live, not because of the people who are evil, but because of the people who don't do anything about it."

Albert Einstein

10

Your 9/11 Moment

Is This Your 9/11 Moment?

On September 11th, 2001, our country, in fact, the entire world, changed forever. When those planes flew into the World Trade Center Twin Towers, there was a worldwide wake-up call. On September 10th, 2001, there were those who suspected there was a problem. However, most people didn't believe it to be as bad as it actually was. In fact, most people were totally unaware of the threat to our society. When those planes crashed into those buildings, there was no doubt we had a massive problem on our hands. It was an undeniable eye-opener, and people were spurred into action.

Life changed for us all on that one fall day. New careers were started as security measures were strengthened. On a federal scale, our homeland security became a renewed priority, and many people joined the military. Not to mention, this tragedy claimed over 3,000 innocent people's lives that day. It's one of those moments that you know exactly where you were when you heard the news and saw those buildings come down.

Time stood still as the unimaginable became reality. The impossible became possible, right before our eyes. We were all forced to reframe our own sense of reality and operate under a new paradigm as we saw replay after replay of this horror. I remember I was driving on Lyons Avenue in Santa Clarita, California, when my wife called and told me what had happened. Where were you?

So now let me ask you, where were you when you learned that child sex trafficking was happening in our country? Where were you when you found out that the average age of entry is a tender 12 years old, and that there could be as many as 300,000 US-born American kids being trafficked for sex in our country right now? Where were you when you learned that kids were being bought and sold for the perverse sexual pleasure of paying "customers" while they are treated like a product rather than a human being? Where were you when you learned that child rape was being allowed to happen in the United States of America? Was it this book? Is it right now?

Is This Your 9/11 Moment?

My hope is that similar to 9/11, readers of this book will be spurred into action and that lives will be changed. My hope is that your world has been forever changed now that you know what you know. Is your reality now reframed? Do you have a new operating paradigm? Personally, I can never go back. I am now destined to commit myself to this important work for the rest of my days. In the words of the British abolitionist, William Wilberforce: "You may choose to look away, but you can never again say you didn't know."

The genie is out of the bottle! So now that you know what you know, what are you going to do? Wilberforce rightly states that we all have a choice. Will you turn a blind eye and go on with your comfortable life? Or will you choose to engage, take it head-on, and be part of the solution that is so desperately needed?

What Can I Do?

I get asked this question all the time: "What can I do?" To which I always reply, "I don't know. What CAN you do?" What do you know? Who do you know? What do they know? What are your skills? What is your education? Who are your friends? What do you do for a living? What can your friends do? Who do they know? Will you introduce them to me?

Here's the deal—we need you to do whatever it is that YOU can do! Also, we need you to go big! We need a massive contribution from you! In fundraising settings, I usually tell the crowd that I would like them to give at an uncomfortable level. We need an extraordinary gift of your time, talent, and treasure to make a difference. I usually let the crowd know that I hope they don't sleep well for at least a week after learning of this problem. That if I saw them a week from now, there would be bags under their eyes from lack of sleep. I can promise you that the kids we serve and the heroes who serve them are living with tension and great discomfort every single day. Our kids are fighting for their very survival every minute of every day. They are being severely violated multiple times a day while staying out all night and oftentimes being physically assaulted in the process.

Somehow, *uncomfortable* does not adequately define it. One of our 15-year-old survivors recently said:

"I had no choice. It was survival."

I've never been in an actual survival situation. I'm not sure I even know what one feels like. I am not afraid to ask anyone for an uncomfortable contribution of their time or resources. Wait, is this turning into a fundraising pitch? Absolutely NOT! I don't want to dumb this down to simple fundraising. That would be easy. I want a piece of your life. I trust that by now your heart has been touched, maybe even pulverized. Good. We need your beat-up heart in this fight. Follow that heart. It will tell you what to do next. My heart drove me in my car to the front door of Saving Innocence. What is yours telling you to do?

Now that you have taken the *red pill*, there is no going back. You can't unsee what you have seen or unlearn what you have learned. A moral conscience, a sense of responsibility, and an authentic masculinity say you must now act. If you think you are too busy to do anything significant, Edmund Burke has something for you to chew on. He said, "Nobody made a greater mistake than he who did nothing because he could only do a little."

You probably have more to give than you think you do. You can't do everything, but you can definitely do something! Whatever it is that you can do, we need you to do it! We need all hands on deck because it all adds up!

Let me remind you of how Bazzel ended his section on *Authentic Masculinity* in Chapter 9.

"When it comes to saving children from trafficking, it is a mission we cannot afford to fail at."

Rachel Thomas, our voice from Chapter 3, gets the final word as she reminds us of the title of this book. I told her recently that her story touched my heart. The fact that she felt trapped in the horrors of sex trafficking and had given up trying to escape breaks my heart. She moved me when she looked *me* in the eye, making me feel as if I was the only one in the auditorium that day, and she said:

"I needed someone to fight for me!"

This lit a fire in my belly and has provided me a lifetime of motivation to continue this fight for her and every victim that desperately needs the same. That concept has ignited my soul and fuels my actions. How can I possibly turn my back on thousands of young girls (and boys) in need of strong men to fight for them? The answer is, I can't. Can you?

My hope and prayer is that you are also a strong man, raising strong men, influencing other men to be strong and that you will also join this fight.

This world and these kids need you! They absolutely need you to fight for them!

Thank you for reading this book. I am honored and encouraged to have you engage with us in this strategic mission and the war on human exploitation for profit.

My prayer is that we have gained a new soldier in the fight against human trafficking. But more than that, that we have gained a strong, powerful man, anxious to live in such a way that he brings to the world healing instead of more wounds, hope instead of despair, and love instead of hate.
Let's go!

Please refer to the appendices where you will find resources, action items, and practical ways to get involved.

"Victory is sweetest when you've known defeat."

Malcolm S. Forbes

"If you're going through hell, keep going."

Winston Churchill

"I can do all things through Christ who strengthens me."

Philippians 4:13

Epilogue
More Than a Survivor
The Best for Last

Many times, I have heard the heart cry of human trafficking survivors. They want to be known for being more than just "a survivor of sex trafficking." Well-meaning reporters and documentarians want to hear the nitty-gritty of their traumatic story because that sells and gets clicks. And I get it. People need to know exactly what is happening out there or else how can we ever expect to fix it? How can you fix something that you don't know is happening? However, our survivor friends want to be known for so much more than simply what happened to them in their past. Don't we all? I would also not want to be labeled and forever known for the hard things in my life, especially for those I had no control over.

I want to end this book strong by sharing the victorious voices of those with actual lived experience. There are several strong women I am in contact with and who also have already contributed to this book. May I not be guilty of the same thing that so many others have been guilty of by only reporting the exploitation and abuse side of their story. These women offer proof that there is hope and a bright future ahead for those still caught in the web of the dehumanizing trauma known as sex trafficking.

I am so honored that these real-life heroes have graciously and enthusiastically added their voices to this book. Many of them told me, "I am so glad you are writing a book for men." For a more complete biography of who they are, what they are doing now, and how to connect with them, please see their bios in Appendix I: "More Than a Survivor" Bios.

When I approached them for this book, I told them that I was not asking them to retell all the hard parts of their story here. They have all done that many times before in various settings. The details of the trafficking part of their story won't be hard to find if you would like to learn more. For this chapter, I asked them just to provide a brief summary of their time in the life to set the stage. At this point, I am most interested in their life after "the life." I asked them each a few questions to guide the conversation. I wanted you to know that each one of these women, like so many others, is most definitely "More Than a Survivor."

Jessica Midkiff

You first met Jessica in Chapter 2, where she courageously shared her personal story of trauma. She then contributed her expertise throughout the rest of the book in order to bring it all to life. Jessica and her daughter have become close to the Smyth family, and we are honored to call her friend.

During your time in the life, what became your perception of men? Of yourself?

My perception of men while I was in the life was that all men wanted sex. They didn't care about my feelings. I believed that they thought that all girls were vessels to be used and abused however they saw fit. I thought all men were tricks and I couldn't trust them. I thought that all men were abusive because that was the norm. I had very few positive males in my life.

After you were able to get out of the life, can you describe the lingering difficulties in those early years, if any?
After leaving the life, I struggled with all types of relationships, trust, self-image, and self-worth. I continued to struggle with my perception of self. I struggled to love myself because I never truly experienced love from others. I still viewed myself as less than because of what I was subjected to for years. It has taken me years to see myself as worthy and priceless. When a few good people came into my life, I didn't know how to trust them. When unhealthy people came into my life, I was in my comfort zone. When I left the life, I was alone, angry, and sad. I was out of place and did not know how to love myself.

Now that you are on the other side of your exploitation, what would you say the key points of your healing have been?
The biggest healing points in my life now are my support system. I am always growing, changing, and finding peace whenever I can. I am gaining an understanding of the difference between trauma and growing pains. If I could make it out of a subculture that is designed to kill a person, not just physically, but mentally, emotionally, and spiritually, I know I can do anything. What helps me to heal daily is having faith and never lying down. Life brings new situations to me every day, and every day I find new ways to keep pushing forward.

I am looking for new and different ways to pour into myself because I realize more and more, every day, that I am worth it.

What are you most grateful for in this part of your life?

I am grateful every day for my life and for sanity. I am grateful for my child. I am grateful for the people that love and care for me. I am grateful that I am able to be a role model for so many people. I am grateful for my voice. I am grateful to have an impact on so many things and people. I am grateful that I am blessed to wake up every day and make great strides in my life. I am grateful because I have great responsibilities in my life. I am grateful because God chose me to do great things in my life, and I hope that I can reach others going forward.

What are some things you are proud of in this part of your life?

I am proud and honored to have been recognized for making contributions in the field of anti-human trafficking. To name a few, I was named Woman of the Year, been a keynote speaker, subject of documentaries, consultant on short films, author of multiple curriculums, and trainer on issues around CSEC [defined and explained in Appendix I: CSEC]. And as you are now aware, I have been blessed to co-write my first book.

What I am most proud of, however, is that I have learned to love, laugh, and cry. I am blessed to be a successful mother to a child sent by God that saved my life. Together we have broken family curses and had some fun along the way. I am in a new season in discovering who I really am and I know I can do it! I will continue to shine, no matter what. I have a purpose and I am unstoppable. I am resilient and I am capable.

Oree Freeman

I have had the honor of working with Oree for two years. She is the life of the party and also a contributor to this book. She is a gifted public speaker on this topic and will move a room into laugher, tears, and action every time.

Can you briefly share the WHAT and HOW of what happened in your exploitation?

You can find elements of my story in Chapter 7. In short, I ran away from home at 11 years old and ended up in the home of a trafficker. He trafficked me in Southern California until I was 15, when a man named Jim helped me escape and find my life again.

During your time in the life, what became your perception of men? Of yourself?

My perception of men was that every man bought sex and that every man was inappropriate. Further, I also thought that every man had a desire to have sex with a child because that was all I ever knew. I had no regard for life, and there was no other way of living. In reality, I feel like I really didn't have any perception of myself. Every single day was consumed with just trying to survive. Because of how I was treated, I had the overall sense that I was worthless. My definition of love was sex, and I viewed myself as an object rather than a person.

After you were able to get out of the life, can you describe the lingering difficulties in those early years, if any?

It is hard to live in the moment now because living in the moment back then was dark and painful. I struggle being present with people, and being alone is the biggest challenge

I have. For the longest time, I didn't know how to live outside of chaos. While in the life, chaos was a way of life, and when the chaos subsided, it was hard to know how to live. I struggle with being patient, and it's hard knowing I am not in control. I am on a journey of redefining trust. Every adult gave me a reason not to trust them while I was in the life. It is difficult to trust adults because of that. There were no healthy relationships in those years, so it continues to be a struggle to build and maintain relationships now.

Now that you are on the other side of your exploitation, what would you say the key points of your healing have been?

The key points to my healing have been entering into a healthy community. My former community was anything but healthy. Also, I have made some unlikely friendships. I have mentors and friends who are white males, which is significant because they resemble a common profile of a typical "John" that I was used to. I have a sisterhood like I never knew existed. Maybe the biggest key to my healing has been that I am in a new environment. Everything is different!

What are you most grateful for in this part of your life?

I am very grateful for the journey of healing that I am on. I see myself making strides and growing stronger every day. I am grateful to be living a true, authentic life. I am grateful for my renewing relationship with God, which is significant to my journey. And most of all, I am grateful to be the mother to my amazing daughter, Evelyn.

What are some things you are proud of in this part of your life?
I think I am most proud of making the decision to heal. It's hard to be on this journey, and it takes a conscious decision to move forward. In order to heal from the kind of trauma I experienced, it takes a focus and intention. It is a constant battle and a daily decision to heal. I am a fighter by nature and proud of the fight that I am in. Additionally, I am proud of being the mother that I am to Eve. It's not easy raising my little girl, but she is so worth it.

What would you say to the men out there who have purchased sex before, in one way or the other? What DON'T they know about the impact of their decisions?
They don't understand the memories we hold. We remember every time we were on our back, and we can't forget a face. These men need to know that their actions have normalized rape and abuse. Before I became a victim, I was a child. I was someone's child with hopes and dreams for a great life. I want these men to understand that their own kids could end up as victims. I want them to know that later in life, I can't define what a healthy relationship looks like. Victims of trafficking become disconnected from our body as a means of coping with the repeated abuse and trauma. They should know that they have turned sex into a thing rather than the beautiful union it was intended to be. The sick memory never goes away. No matter how much you heal, it's always there. The database inside you of all the past never goes away.

If the ultimate goal is to end human trafficking—and it is, what are some bullet-point actions we should take in order to end it?
We need to impact communities that are lacking resources because this is where the majority of victims come from. We need to focus on generational curses because so much of this trauma is passed down within a family. Better schools will empower the vulnerable and provide more opportunities in life. Critical in ending trafficking is getting more men as positive role models. We need to help the privileged know they can do something about it and then show them how. We need to create better support systems for survivors after they are out of the life. We need to empower the next generation of young boys and show them a healthy path for their life. Redefining success for men will be key to this process.

Nola Brantley
Nola will command a full room with her passion, energy, and humor as she provides human trafficking trainings all over the country through her organization, Nola Brantley Speaks. She is based in Los Angeles, so I am privileged to interact with her now and then.

Can you briefly share the WHAT and HOW of what happened in your exploitation?
I came from a broken home where we lived in extreme poverty, and there were no positive male role models present in my life. I had a history of sexual abuse that dated back to before I could walk or talk. I was a sophomore in high school when I was targeted by a school police officer who turned out to be my perpetrator. I didn't realize I was being victimized, and I was

just happy to have his attention and to have access to things that poverty did not allow me to have access to throughout my life. I was 15 and he was 35!

During your time in the life, what became your perception of men? Of yourself?

My perception of men became that they all wanted to have sex with me! That men had no control over their sexual desires and that made them weak. That many men were sexually sick! I thought that people valued me most based on sex. I thought sex was the most valuable thing I had to offer this world. I thought I was put on this earth to satisfy people sexually.

After you were able to get out of the life, can you describe the lingering difficulties in those early years, if any?

Those areas that had been damaged from early childhood sexual abuse had not been restored. As a result, I was not able to connect the dots between the things that happened to me during my early childhood and my current behaviors and choices in life. After being in the life, I ended up in a domestic violence relationship with a man who began beating me when I became pregnant and almost took my life. The areas that had been damaged caused me to link love, sex, and abuse. Furthermore, I was full of guilt and shame from the things that happened to me, and I viewed myself more as a sexual object than anything else, and my self-esteem was very low.

Now that you are on the other side of your exploitation, what would you say the key points of your healing have been?

The key points of my healing have been to surround myself with people who accept me for who I am and to understand where I am at in my journey of healing and recovery. Another key point has been to surround myself with people who are good role models for what it means to live a healthy and fulfilled life. It has also been very important for me to learn to forgive and accept myself for who I am, including the things that have happened to me and the things I desire to change. I have also learned that given my past, it is important for me to stay continuously engaged in some type of therapeutic services. Lastly, nature is my friend and helps to heal me and teach me about myself.

What are you most grateful for in this part of your life?
Freedom! The chance to get it right! Jesus Christ as my friend and personal savior! My family, all of them! Abundance! Life! Mobility! My puppies! Healthy love! The opportunity to contribute to the world in a meaningful way! Friendships! Provisions! God's grace!!!

What are some things you are proud of in this part of your life?
I am proud that I was able to establish MISSSEY [Motivating, Inspiring, Supporting, and Serving Sexually Exploited Youth; www.missey.org] and provide leadership for that organization for seven years. It was one of the first community-based organizations in California to begin to offer services to commercially sexually exploited children and youth, and it was a model for many other organizations that began to emerge across the nation. I am also proud I was able to establish Nola Brantley Speaks!, an organization that offers training, education, and event coordination across the state of California and the nation on topics related to the commercial sexual exploitation of children and youth.

Through Nola Brantley Speaks!, we have been able to establish a training model where we match clinicians with commercially sexually exploited children and youth with survivors of the commercial sex industry. This model has been amazing and provides multidisciplinary audiences across the state with both a clinical lens and a lived experience practical view of the topic. I am also very proud of my role within my family and my relationships with my children! I continue to face my own personal challenges, and I am proud of myself for continuing to have the courage to march forward.

What would you say to the men out there who have purchased sex before, in one way or the other? What DON'T they know about the impact of their decisions?

I would say to these men, value yourself more than this decision! You deserve true intimacy with someone who loves you, cares about you, and wants to get to know you more than just have sex with you. Sex should be a bonus with someone who already makes you feel good in other ways. Sometimes we settle for sex when we can't have a true connection to help satisfy our loneliness. Or sometimes we have sex because we have very strong physical needs. Take the time to find people and make true connections with them. Somebody will want to make a connection with you.

If the ultimate goal is to end human trafficking—and it is, what are some bullet-point actions we should take in order to end it?

In order to end human trafficking, we would need to address the core issues that create the vulnerabilities. To begin with, these core issues are poverty, racism, sexism, classism. At the end of the day, if folks want to end something as enormous as human trafficking, they're not going to be able to live their lives in the status quo. In order to create more equanimity throughout the world, we have to be willing to make sacrifices because there is enough for everybody to be okay. In this world, some people have more than enough resources and some people have nothing. As long as it's that way, then we will always have individuals throughout the world who will be victims of human trafficking.

Rachel Thomas

You met Rachel in Chapter 3. I told her that her story touched my heart because it made the crime of human trafficking relevant to every dad in America. "I needed someone to fight for me" still gets me every time. Rachel founded a great organization focused on awareness and empowerment of survivors called The Sowers Education Group, and she created a phenomenal prevention tool that every single teen should watch called *The Cool Aunt* series.

Can you briefly share the WHAT and HOW of what happened in your exploitation?

I will defer you to Chapter 3 of this book where I go into detail describing the what and the how of my exploitation. If you haven't read that chapter, please do so now!

During your time in the life, what became your perception of men? Of yourself?

During this time of my life, my perception of men was that they were predatory. They felt unsafe to be around, and they were always expecting something of me—sexually, financially, to stroke their ego, or fulfill whatever whim. I lived a very stressful, walking-on-eggshells type of existence all the time. I was most definitely in survival mode, doing whatever I needed to do to stay alive that day.

After you were able to get out of the life, can you describe the lingering difficulties in those early years, if any?
I would say the biggest lingering difficulty was my perception of myself. I battled the persistent feeling that I was to blame for getting into that situation and that I was damaged goods because of it. I had mixed emotions about seeing myself as a victim. It was disempowering because it meant that I was taken advantage of and abused, yet it also meant that it was not my fault or my shame to carry.

Additional lingering difficulties included just simply trying to understand how all this happened to me. Simply trying to make sense of it all was hard. Romantic relationships were a struggle, and sexual intimacy immediately brought back flashbacks of trauma.

Now that you are on the other side of your exploitation, what would you say the key points of your healing have been?
The key point to my healing is definitely my spirituality. Understanding God's love and being able to believe and receive that love is critical, especially if you don't have a lot of great examples of human love.

Another key component to my healing has been to gain an in-depth understanding of coercion. Because of that, I understand exactly how I was manipulated, and I am confident that it won't ever happen again. I now feel empowered to not only stay safe from manipulators but to help others do the same.

Finally, it was important for me to develop an identity outside of the life. This was pretty easy for me because I already had an identity. My exploitation did not begin until I was 19 years old, so I had a life to return to. Immediately after I exited my trafficking experience, I was able to step back into being a student. I threw myself back into school and allowed my study, reading, and assignments to occupy my mind.

What are you most grateful for in this part of your life?
Every day, I am more and more grateful for my family, my parents, and my support system. All my best friends are my safety net. I am grateful for being stable emotionally, financially, and spiritually.

What are some things you are proud of in this part of your life?
I am very proud of the prevention curriculum I created called "Ending the Game." I have heard from many women that it has been life changing for them. There have been over a thousand survivors who have gone through it. This makes my heart happy because it helps me to find something positive about my experiences in that I can now help others find their way out.

I am very proud of my son. He is an amazing, happy, smart, kind little boy. And most definitely a source of pure joy for me. I'm also grateful for the good and healthy relationship I have with his father. Even though our marriage didn't work out, I'm grateful that we let love lead and we're still both dedicated to doing what's best for Emory.

What would you say to the men out there who have purchased sex before, in one way or the other? What DON'T they know about the impact of their decisions?
I would want them to know that they are contributing to the larger problem of a broken world. The buyer needs to know

that he is hurting whomever he has bought like a product and preventing them from ever becoming the full capacity of what they were truly put on this earth to be.

I would also want him to know that his actions are decreasing his own chances of ever having a fulfilling relationship and that he's harming his ability to become the full, healthy man he is supposed to be and that this world needs.

If the ultimate goal is to end human trafficking—and it is, what are some bullet-point actions we should take in order to end it?

There is so much to say here. I would say the most strategic thing we could do is to somehow strengthen all family systems. The strengthening of families would go a long way in reducing the crime of human trafficking. As part of that effort, we need to create more opportunities for men of color.

A close relative to creating stronger families is to pour more resources and energy into creating a better foster care system. We need more focus put on finding and training better foster parents along with enough checks and balances to keep the system safe for vulnerable kids.

We need more churches stepping up to empower and equip families for the tough task at hand.

We know that this crime is driven by economics. So the presence of poverty is a major contributing force in motivating human trafficking. To that end, a major focus on economic systems and the financial empowerment of poor people is necessary. Creating more opportunities for meaningful work for both young men and young women is critical.

For those who are already down this path, creating much stricter penalties for traffickers and buyers and more focused anti-trafficking units will act as a deterrent.

We also need to address our overly sexualized society. It seems that every billboard, song, or advertisement is selling sex and the objectification of women. We are training our kids on what to do and what to expect with the everyday, normal environment they are growing up in.

Harmony Dust Grillo

Harmony tells the in-depth version of her story in her book, *Scars & Stilettos*. She founded and runs an important organization called Treasures, which is focused on girls trapped in the sex industry. I have heard her speak and train several times, and she is outstanding in that role.

Can you briefly share the WHAT and HOW of what happened in your exploitation?

I was raised in a chaotic home in a neighborhood run by gangs and riddled with violence. Beginning at the age of five, my childhood was also marked by sexual abuse at the hands of multiple people.

At thirteen, my mother left me and my eight-year-old brother for a summer to fend for ourselves with nothing but twenty dollars and a book of food stamps. I became susceptible to a relationship with an older boy who bought us food and told me he would take care of us. The relationship became toxic, abusive, and ultimately exploitative. I began working in a strip club at the age of nineteen, and my abusive "boyfriend" became my pimp, controlling my every move and taking all of my money.

Ultimately, I found a path to freedom and a whole new life. Thankfully, all of the pain from my past is being used today to help others.

During your time in the life, what became your perception of men? Of yourself?
There was a time when I absolutely hated men. Based on my history of trauma, I genuinely believed that all men were inherently perverted and abusive. I plastered on a smile in the strip clubs, but inside, I was seething with rage. When men would violate my boundaries, I would retaliate by taking off my stiletto and beating them in the head. Toward the end of my time in the sex industry, I began looking for any reason to lash out. It didn't take much to set me off.

Being treated like nothing more than a sexual object, day in and day out, left me feeling dead inside. I was a shell of a person.

The sex industry is built on fantasy. Fantasy says, "This is who I want you to be." Intimacy says, "I want to know and be known by you."

Who I was didn't matter. I became whoever the customer paid me to be. Eventually, I lost sight of who I was.

After you were able to get out of the life, can you describe the lingering difficulties in those early years, if any?
One of the most obvious challenges was finances. I had a gap in my resume and no real marketable job skills. I ended up taking a job working in a group home, making just over minimum wage. As hard as that was, I felt so free and empowered to finally make money doing something that didn't involve selling myself.

169

Leaving the commercial sex industry meant having to engage in a complete life overhaul, from my job to the "boy-friend" to all of my social relationships and even relationship patterns.

When you think about it, ending a romantic relationship is hard. Ending a friendship is hard. Leaving a job is hard. Leaving the life means doing all of this at once. And on top of all of that, having to face and deal with all of the trauma from before and during my time in the sex industry.

Facing the pain and trauma of my past and how it has impacted my life and choices had been an ongoing process. This has looked different in different seasons. Initially, it took everything in me to gain the courage to deal with the sexual abuse and rape I experienced. It was so daunting to me at one point, I thought it was impossible to get past it. Today, I know that I am free from the grip my past had on me, but I am not done learning and growing. I am committed to the process of becom-ing all that I was created to be until the day I take my last breath.

Now that you are on the other side of your exploitation, what would you say the key points of your healing have been?
Facing the pain. Because we can't heal a wound by saying it's not there (Jer. 6:14 TLB), and we cannot fix what we do not face.

Because I didn't deal with the pain, the pain had a way of dealing with me. Often, our misdirected efforts to cope with pain lead us into deeper places of despair. Attempts to escape pain can create unhealthy patterns such as overeating, alco-hol or drug dependency, eating disorders, self-harm, or even binging on Netflix in an attempt to avoid reality.

We must face our pain to overcome it. It's not easy, but it's worth it.

Breaking the silence. Doing this is a catalyst for healing. I have heard it said that we are as sick as our secrets. My secrets made me sick. They kept me isolated and afraid of getting too close to people for fear of them seeing who I really was behind the masks I wore. My voice, my ability to tell the truth about what I had been through, was stifled by the looming feeling and false belief that if I spoke up, something really bad would happen. When I finally broke the silence, I discovered that I was not alone in my pain. And I experienced incredible breakthroughs.

Replacing the lies. A long history of abuse led me to believe that I was the kind of girl who deserved to be abused. It shaped the way I viewed myself and the world around me and kept me stuck in destructive relationships. Transformation and healing often require a makeover of the mind. It is up to us to actively identify and take hold of the lies we believe and replace them with the truth.

Doing the hard work of forgiveness. Forgiveness is setting someone free and realizing the prisoner was you. Forgiveness was a vital part of my healing journey. Forgiveness isn't endorsement, and it certainly isn't accompanied by warm, fuzzy feelings. Forgiveness is a choice we make. Releasing the people who have done wrong to us by forgiving them isn't always easy, but it is good.

What are you most grateful for in this part of your life?
I am most grateful for a healthy marriage and family that is committed to loving each other through action. And we have a lot of fun in the process!

What are some things you are proud of in this part of your life?

I actually feel more humbled than proud of what I have accomplished in the area of my calling, career, and the pursuit of justice.

What I am most proud of is that I have a daughter who feels safe enough to come to me with her true feelings, authentic self, and biggest challenges and questions in life. I am also proud of having an emotionally healthy marriage and the fact that I genuinely like the woman I am today as well as the woman I am becoming.

What would you say to the men out there who have purchased sex before, in one way or the other? What DON'T they know about the impact of their decisions?

Men, we need you to do whatever it takes to get free. There are people on the other end of your freedom. Men and boys who need your voice and influence. Women and girls who need you to rise up and take your place as protectors and defenders of dignity. We can't see an end to the injustice of exploitation without you.

If the ultimate goal is to end human trafficking—and it is, what are some actions we should take in order to end it?

We need to engage in efforts to End demand.

Protect the vulnerable, for example, through fostering and adopting programs for at-risk youth and their families, etc.

Provide effective services and support to survivors so they can rebuild their life and end generational cycles.

Rebecca Bender

Rebecca is also on this list and contributed to this book. However, she is unable to share about her personal life due to contractual obligations with other projects she is working on. You can pick up her book, *In Pursuit of Love,* where she goes into great detail on her incredible triumph. She is a powerful voice of victory and hope.

There they are, everyone! Some truly strong and resilient women who rose above their trauma and are now working hard to make the world a better place. They are turning pain into power and providing a way of escape to the next generation by being an example of what is possible. I am truly grateful and honored that they contributed to this book.

Please see their bios in Appendix G: "More Than a Survivor" Bios. Visit their websites, follow their social media, and buy their books! They are worth following!

Table of Contents for Appendices

Appendix A: How to Report Human Trafficking 177
Appendix B: Contact Information 179
Appendix C: Warning Signs of Human Trafficking 181
Appendix D: Things You Can Do Today! 183
Appendix E: Things Your Church Can Do 185
Appendix F: Resources for Pornography Addiction 193
Appendix G: "More Than a Survivor" Bios 195
Appendix H: Recommended Resources 204
   Prevention—*The Cool Aunt* Series 204
   Sex + Money Documentary 205
   Recommended Books 206
Appendix I: CSEC 207
Appendix J: The Man in the Arena 210

Contributors 211
Acknowledgments 213
Notes 217
About the Authors 221

Appendix A

To Report A Tip or Connect with Anti-Trafficking Services in Your Area

National Human Trafficking Hotline
1-888-373-7888 (TTY: 711)
*Text 233733
The National Human Trafficking Resource Center (NHTRC) is a national, toll-free hotline, available to answer calls from anywhere in the country, 24 hours a day, 7 days a week, every day of the year.

National Center for Missing & Exploited Children
1-800-843-5678 (1-800-THE-LOST)
If you have information about a missing child or suspected child sexual exploitation, call to report it or visit their website, www.missingkids.com/cybertipline

The National Runaway Safeline
1-800-786-2929 (1-800-RUNAWAY)
The National Runaway Safeline serves as the federally designated national communication system for homeless and

runaway youth. Through hotline and online services, NRS provides crisis intervention, referrals to local resources, and education and prevention services to youth, families, and community members throughout the country 24 hours a day, 365 days a year.

If you see or suspect an active abduction
Call 911

Appendix B
Contact Information

Men! Fight For Me:
The Role of Authentic Masculinity in Ending Sexual
Exploitation and Trafficking
To order more books, follow our blog and stay in the know:

Website: www.fightforme.net
Hashtag #fightformebook

Social Media:
Instagram: @fightformebook
Facebook: Fight For Me Book
Twitter: @2Cor618—"Fight For Me Book"
YouTube: Fight For Me

Alan Smyth:
E-mail: alansmyth1981@gmail.com
Instagram: @smythalan
Facebook: Alan Smyth
Twitter: @alansmyth81

Speaking:
To Inquire about having us speak to your group, contact Alan
Smyth: alansmyth1981@gmail.com

Appendix C
Warning Signs of Human Trafficking

Warning Signs of an Individual Being Trafficked:[21]
Signs of physical abuse such as burn marks, bruises, or cuts
Unexplained absences from class
Less appropriately dressed than before
Sexualized behavior
Overly tired in class
Withdrawn, depressed, distracted, or checked out
Brags about making or having lots of money
Less appropriately dressed than before or new expensive clothes, accessories, or shoes
New tattoo (tattoos are often used by pimps as a way to brand victims)
Tattoos of a name, symbol of money, or barcode could indicate trafficking
Older boyfriend or new friends with a different lifestyle
Talks about wild parties, or invites other students to attend parties
Shows signs of gang affiliation (a preference for specific colors, display gang symbols)

Pimps/Traffickers Often Exhibit the Following Behaviors or Characteristics:
Jealous, controlling, and violent
Significantly older than female companions
Promise things that seem too good to be true
Encourage victims to engage in illegal activities to achieve their goals and dreams
Buys expensive gifts or owns expensive items
Is vague about his/her profession
Pushy or demanding about sex
Encourages inappropriate sexual behavior
Makes the victim feel responsible for his/her financial stability.
Very open about financial matters

Appendix D
Things You Can Do Today!

1. Become more educated on all things human trafficking.
2. Follow anti-human trafficking work on social media. Start with @savinginnocence
3. From social media, look for items to share, like, or retweet.
4. From your social media, post what you are learning about human trafficking to raise awareness.
5. Visit the websites of your local human trafficking agencies. Start with www.savinginnocence.org.
6. Become a financial donor to local anti-human trafficking efforts.
7. Check to see if your employer will match donations.
8. Find out what your church is doing about human trafficking.
9. Gather gift cards and other tangible items and distribute them to anti-human trafficking organizations.
10. Use smile.amazon.com to make all of your Amazon purchases. Select "Saving Innocence" as your charity of choice if you don't already have one.
11. Read the books found on the "Recommended Books" list in this book (Appendix H).

12. Watch *Nefarious: Merchant of Souls*, produced by Exodus Cry.
13. Buy the video series *The Cool Aunt* for every teen in your life.
    Visit www.thecoolauntseries.com to purchase it.
14. Figure out whatever else you can do...then DO IT!
15. E-mail, text, or call ten friends and ask them to do all of the above.

Appendix E
Things Your Church Can Do

To My Faith-Based Crowd

This book is strategically "faith neutral" for most of its content. The reason is that I wanted to include as many men in this conversation as possible. I did not want to make anyone feel disqualified from the conversation because of their faith perspective or lack thereof. A particular personal faith is not necessary for motivation to join this battle. Justice and freedom for children are universal values that all humans can support and fight for. Having said that, if you are connected to a faith community, please do everything you can to bring your church, parish, or synagogue into this fight.

Jesus was very clear on his opinion of children in Matthew 19:14:

"Let the little children come to me, and do not hinder them, for the kingdom of heaven belongs to such as these."

Jesus is letting us know where children rank in his view. He clearly is sending the message that kids are a subject of his affection and protection. Further, he is letting us know that heaven has a special place for children. Kids are high on his priority list.

The Bible goes on to clarify God's position on this topic in Psalms 11:7:

"For the Lord is righteous, and loves justice."

It's hard to imagine something more unjust than a child being repeatedly bought and sold for sex through no fault of their own. Clearly, this is something that God detests. If this is important to God, then it should be important to those who follow him. We should be growing closer to Christ as we continue to follow him, and therefore, more and more of our actions should reflect more and more of his heart. His agenda should be our agenda. That is how the Christian life is supposed to work!

In Luke 4:18, we receive our marching orders as Jesus reveals his:

"The spirit of the Lord is on me, because He has anointed me to proclaim good news to the poor. He has sent me to proclaim freedom for the prisoners ... to set the oppressed free."

Jesus is declaring that these are his goals. As we become more like Jesus, our actions begin to imitate his. And our thoughts begin to mimic his. In short, his marching orders become our marching orders as we become more like Jesus. This seems clear to me. As followers of Jesus, we are supposed to somehow give ourselves to bringing good news and freedom to oppressed children because he loves justice.

Ephesians 6:12 reminds us where the ultimate battles are being fought:

"For our battle is not against flesh and blood."

People of faith would point to a spiritual battle in the unseen places as a major factor of human trafficking. We have to bring this fight to every corner of humanity, including the spiritual realm.

To the worldwide church, regardless of denomination or perspective, we not only need you to contribute from your vast resources to this fight, but we need you to join in the spiritual battle as well. Most people, regardless of faith, have a concept of good and evil. You know it when you see it. I can personally attest to what I have seen and heard firsthand that the crime of child sex trafficking is pure evil running amuck.

When I hear of a 16-year-old being sold by her own father to a drug dealer for $200,000 only after raping her, because the buyer "didn't want to have any virgins..."

When I hear of an 8-year-old being sold over and over starting at age 4...

When I hear of a mother selling her own 11-year-old daughter to pay for drugs...

When I interact with survivors who were forced to be out on the streets at 11 years old and being raped 15 times every single night...

I'm no theologian, but I would say that all of the above is pure evil by anyone's definition. I could go on, but you get the idea. The exploitation and dehumanization of women and children have thus far been the devil's playground. He has had free rein, and it's time for the church to show up, stand up, and resist in a powerful way.

We need the church to engage in this battle at every level. And we know that "the church" is not the building you meet in. The church is God's people, one by one, gathering, mobilizing, and effecting change in a broken world.

We have victory in Christ. The ultimate battle has already been won. It's time to rise up and assert God's power and authority. Edmund Burke has an important reminder for us when he says the following:

"The only thing necessary for the triumph of evil is
for good men to do nothing."

If you consider yourself part of God's church and one of his followers, then I am calling you into action against human trafficking and into an all-out, scorched-earth, ground war waged against the evil one and his schemes. I honestly can't imagine something higher on God's to-do list than eradicating this atrocity against his children. Can you?

Here are two questions for the leadership of your faith community:

1. What is our strategy to be part of the solution to human trafficking?
   If they have a good answer, ask how you can join the team.
   If they don't have an answer, proceed with question two.
2. Why are we not an active part of this fight? It seems like we should be.

If the answer is, "We are just learning about this and we need someone to take leadership," great—volunteer to help lead the effort.

If the answer is, "We've looked at it, and we really don't think it's important enough to allocate time and energy to. We have no plans to partner with an anti-human trafficking effort."

They would never actually say it like that. You would pick that up more from their actions. I guess you would then be faced with a predicament and would have to figure out your next move and whether or not that is a church you can continue to attend.

I am fully aware that many churches are underfunded and understaffed, and yours may be faced with that same problem. However, I believe this evil injustice is something we simply can't ignore or turn a blind eye to because we are overworked and consumed with other initiatives and programs. There are many important issues, but I firmly believe an injustice like this requires a reprioritization of your church's assets if we are to win this battle!

The lives of children in your community (and maybe your church) depend on it. The soul of humanity is hanging in the balance, and the kingdom of heaven weeps because of it.

I wanted to make sure that the above challenge actually resonated with the actual church. I asked my friend Bruce Garner, author of *The Resilient Pastor* and the senior pastor of CrossPoint Church in Huntington Beach, California, if he would give this a read and provide his feedback. I told him that while the bulk of the book is strategically "faith neutral," I definitely wanted the larger church to engage. I am hoping that guys like Bruce (church pastors) will grab hold of this book and lead their congregations accordingly. His feedback is below:

I think it's very good.

One thing to understand about the psychology of decision makers, especially senior pastors, is that we get enlisted to do more things than we can possibly do, and that happens all the time. So I think it would be worth your while to acknowledge that, and then say that this actually is different. It's different precisely because it is so horrifying. Very few other people will do it, and short of heaven and hell, there is nothing on earth more heartbreaking and horrifying that they could possibly invest in.

I think a perfect biblical appeal can be found in Proverbs 24:10-12:

"If you falter in a time of trouble, how small is your strength!

Rescue those being led away to death; hold back those staggering toward slaughter.

If you say, "But we knew nothing about this," does not he who weighs the heart perceive it? Does not he who guards your life know it?

Will he not repay everyone according to what they have done?"

I would quickly follow that up with an appeal to do something right now, even if it's small. You and I both know that getting started is the hardest thing for new volunteers or donors. Ask them to do at least one small thing, then you start telling the stories and showing the value, and I just have to believe that they will do more as time goes on.

Well said, Bruce! Thank you for leading your church in such meaningful ways. Following Bruce's suggestion above, please find below some immediate action items that you and your church can get started with. Also, in Appendix D, you will find a list of "Things You Can Do Today." Let's get started right away. There is no time to waste!

"In the same way, faith by itself, if it not accompanied by action, is dead."
James 2:17

Action Items:
Here are some practical action items that your church can consider doing:

1. Include anti-human trafficking efforts and agencies in your church prayer strategy.
2. Add anti-human trafficking work to your church budget. Look for a local organization and, in lieu of that, please visit www.savinginnocence.org for a worthy giving option.
3. Add human trafficking to your annual communication from the pulpit, bringing awareness of this crime to your congregation.
4. Bless local anti-human trafficking agencies at Christmas (or anytime). Gifts for the advocates and gifts for the survivors are very much appreciated.

5. Collect tangible items and distribute them to your local organizations. Find out what the need is and then meet that need. Assorted gift cards are always appreciated.

6. Invite a human trafficking expert to speak at your church.

7. Create a strategy to reach single moms. As part of that strategy, mobilize healthy men to be available to their kids.

8. Make sure your youth outreach staff is thinking about the furthest-out kids who are in the most need. They are the ones most vulnerable to human trafficking.

Start small. Consider an annual drive of some kind. Gathering practical items such as food, personal hygiene items, blankets, and needed clothing is always a great idea. An annual gift card drive for food items, fast-food, coffee, or food delivery services is always appreciated. Christmas gifts for survivors and gifts for their young children are incredibly meaningful. Basically, you can't go wrong. Pick something and get started. Let it grow from there.

Appendix F:
Resources for Pornography
Addiction

My friend Benji Nolot is the founder and executive director of an impactful organization called Exodus Cry. Years ago, he produced the groundbreaking documentary on trafficking called *Nefarious: Merchant of Souls.* He has many other great accomplishments to his credit. Among them is a powerful documentary on pornography called *Beyond Fantasy.* Please find it and watch it.

He recently said this about pornography:

What does pornography teach us about sex? In pornography, sex is cast as a vehicle for the destruction of women, for the pleasure of men. Plain and simple.

What does pornography teach women? Pornography educates females about the scope of violating and humiliating sexual scenarios they will be expected to comply with, under the guise of "liberating" and "empowering" sexual experience. It teaches them to internalize the sexual trauma wreaked upon them on a sexually hostile planet as something fun, erotic, kinky, and sexy.

What does pornography teach men? Pornography educates males about the scope of aggression and domination that is expected of them in sexual scenarios in order to punish, degrade, and violate women under the guise of "being a real man."

If you or someone you know is struggling with pornography, please see the following resources:

www.fightthenewdrug.org—Providing scientific research to help you make informed decisions about pornography use.

www.covenanteyes.com—Helps you set up accountability partners.

www.opendns.com—Provides tools for parents to block pornography on home Wi-Fi.

Appendix G
"More Than a Survivor" Bios

Oree Freeman

Oree lives a life of service. She is a woman who has overcome adversity and continues to thrive through life's many twists and turns. Oree is passionate, filled with spunk, and is tenacious in her advocacy. Oree's mission is to be a voice and a fighter for all victims of sex trafficking, and she has devoted her career to combating sex trafficking by establishing AWARENESS, spreading HOPE, and helping others find RESILIENCE within themselves. Over 25,000 individuals have felt her strength through the interactive training she conducts for law enforcement officers and professionals from other child-serving sectors. Importantly, she has also focused her energy on working directly with exploited and at-risk youth.

Oree is an advocate where she transforms the lives of youth involved in the juvenile justice and child welfare systems by sharing what she has learned from her own experience as well as the countless youth she has served over the past eight years. Oree is a survivor not only of child sex trafficking but a survivor of life's unfair battles, and she remains Undefeated. She lives a life of service, and this is just the beginning of her journey. She is Unstoppable.

Consultation: Curriculum development, advocacy for young girls, Media marketing, CSEC 101
www.oreefreeman.com

Social Media
Instagram: OreeFreeman
Podcast: ANCHORED
Services Offered:
Training:
1. The Power of Connection and Unlikely Relationships
2. "It's gotta cost you something" (reviving the team within an organization)

Harmony (Dust) Grillo

Survivor of exploitation turned UCLA honor student, Harmony's goal is to help women and girls entrenched in sexual exploitation find freedom.

Armed with personal experience, evidence-based theories, and a master's of social work degree, she comprehensively sheds light on the impact of a pornified culture and the lives of those trapped within it. Her pursuit of justice has led to congressional recognition and opportunities to train the Department of Justice and the FBI in best practices. In 2003, she founded Treasures to empower other women in their recovery and freedom from the commercial sex industry and trafficking.

Harmony's memoir, *Scars & Stilettos*, details her harrowing account of moving from victim to survivor to liberator.

Website:

www.iamatreasure.com

Social Media:
Instagram, Facebook, and Twitter:
@TreasuresLA
@HarmonyGrillo

Description of Harmony's memoir, *Scars & Stilettos*:
At thirteen, after being abandoned by her mother one summer and left to take care of her younger brother, Harmony
becomes susceptible to a relationship that turns out to be
toxic, abusive, and ultimately exploitative. She eventually finds
herself working in a strip club at the age of nineteen, and her
boyfriend becomes her pimp, controlling her every move and
taking all of her money. Ultimately, she discovers a path to
freedom and a whole new life.

Rachel Thomas
Appointed member of the United States Advisory Council on
Human Trafficking

A graduate of UCLA with a master's in education and a personal survivor of human trafficking, Rachel has extensive experience teaching, training, curriculum writing, public speaking, and mentoring. As the founder of Sowers Education Group and the lead author of the "Ending The Game" curriculum and *The Cool Aunt* series, she has educated and inspired a wide range of audiences, including teens, social service providers, churches, teachers, college students, and law enforcement. Sowers' intervention curriculum, "Ending The Game," is being used by over 1,000 facilitators in 36 states to help survivors break the bonds of attachment to traffickers and the lifestyle of commercial sexual exploitation.

Rachel was not only honored by Congressman Ed Royce of California's 39th district and Los Angeles Supervisor Don Knabe for her leadership and trafficking prevention efforts, but she was also nominated and appointed to the White House Advisory Council on Human Trafficking for the 2020-2022 term.

Organizations: Sowers Education Group and Ending The Game

Mission and Vision: To sow seeds of awareness about human trafficking and survivor empowerment.

Websites:
www.EndingTheGame.com
www.SowersEducationgroup.com
www.coolauntseries.com

Social Media:
Instagram: @RachelThomasWasHere
Facebook: @RachelCThomas

Nola Brantley

Nola Brantley Speaks

Nola Brantley is best known publicly as a nationally acclaimed advocate who has played a large role in spearheading the Domestic Minor Sex Trafficking /Commercial Sexual Exploitation of Children (DMST/CSEC) awareness and advocacy movement in the state of California since 2001. Nola is a mother, an activist against all forms of social injustice, a motivational speaker, a woman of color, a survivor, a sister, and a visionary.

Mission and Vision:

Advocating for a more empowered world for all human beings.

Nola Brantley Speaks exists to empower a community of advocates through training, curriculum development, and event coordination and to create a community of support for individuals exiting and currently in the commercial sex industry.

Values:
EMPOWERMENT: Empowerment of all human beings is essential for society to thrive.
CHILDHOOD: Childhood is precious and should be protected.
RELATIONSHIP: Healing and restoration occur in the context of relationships.
RESILIENCY: Survivors of abuse have strength and courage beyond measure.

Website:
www.nolabrantleyspeaks.org

Shopify:
Nola-brantley-speaks.myshopify.com

Social Media:
Instagram: nolabrantleyspeaks
Facebook: Empowerwomenandgirls
Twitter: brantley_speaks
Clubhouse: nbspeaks

Follow:
#care4selfcare4others

Rebecca Bender, MACT
CEO and founder of the Rebecca Bender Initiative
Author of *In Pursuit of Love* and *Roadmap to Redemption*

Relentless in her mission to help others find their purpose, Rebecca Bender is the CEO of the Rebecca Bender Initiative and founder of Elevate Academy, the largest online school for survivors of trafficking in the world. An award-winning thought leader, advocate, author, and consultant, she provides education on many human trafficking-related topics and serves the US Department of State Advisory Council on Human Trafficking as well as advises a variety of nonprofits.

Rebecca has trained well over 100,000 professionals, including FBI, Homeland Security, local law enforcement, vice units, and medical personnel. In 2017, Rebecca was selected as one of twenty-one representative members on the National Advisory Committee on Sex Trafficking of Children and Youth in the United States. The committee advises the Department of Health and Human Services and the Attorney General on policies concerning improvements to the nation's response to the sex trafficking of children and youth.

Website:
www.rebeccabender.org

Appendix H
Recommended Resources

The Cool Aunt
SEX TRAFFICKING TALK
WITH AUNTIE RACHEL

The Cool Aunt Series: Sex Trafficking Prevention for Teens is more than an online course, it's an experience. Using engaging and age-appropriate cinema, storytelling, lecture, and questions, the series walks teens through the STREAMS of Influence—the seven risk factors that lead to sex trafficking: Survival, Trafficker, Recruiter, Environment, Abuse, Media, Solicitation. After the series, teens have the opportunity to self-assess their risk factors and get one-on-one help if needed. *The Cool Aunt Experience* has been called "powerful," "amazing," "fun," and "lifesaving" by teens, caregivers, and anti-trafficking experts.

Website:
www.TheCoolAuntSeries.com
Instagram:
@TheCoolAuntSeries

Lot 3 Productions, in partnership with Saving Innocence, brings you:

Sex + Money: A National Search for Human Worth. Sex + Money is a documentary about the shocking reality of domestic minor sex trafficking in the United States and the rising movement of advocates fighting to abolish it.

How did commercial sexual exploitation become the nation's fastest-growing criminal enterprise? What can be done to stop it? The film crew traveled to over 30 states to make the documentary and conducted more than 75 interviews with federal agents, survivors, former traffickers, politicians, leading activists, psychologists, pornographers, and many others.

To learn about how to watch the film and join the impact campaign, go to: www.sexandmoneyfilm.com.

Recommended Books

In Pursuit of Love: One Woman's Journey from Trafficked to Triumphant, by Rebecca Bender, published by Zondervan (Grand Rapids, MI), 2020

Scars & Stilettos: The Transformation of an Exotic Dancer, 2nd Ed., by Harmony Dust, published by Monarch Books (Los Angeles, CA), 2017

Advocacy for Commercially Sexually Exploited Youth, by Nola Brantley-Harris and Nicole Klasey, PsyD

Girls Like Us: Fighting for a World Where Girls Are Not for Sale, by Rachel Lloyd, published by Harper Perennial (New York, NY), 2012

Raising a Modern-Day Knight: A Father's Role in Guiding His Son to Authentic Manhood, by Robert Lewis, published by Tyndale House Publishers (Carol Stream, IL), 2007

How You Can Fight Human Trafficking:100 Ways to Make a Difference, by Through God's Grace/Susan Patterson, published by Through God's Grace Ministry (Irvine, CA), 2014

Prized Possession: A Father's Journey in Raising His Daughter, by Alan Smyth and Kristy Fox, published by AuthorHouse (Bloomington, IN), 2013

Appendix I
CSEC—The Acronym

Every business, company, or sector has a number of acronyms they use. Acronyms provide an immediate understanding of commonly used concepts and principles. They expedite communication and provide instant connection to the issues being discussed.

On my first day at Saving Innocence, I learned about a commonly used acronym. It's probably the most used and commonly understood acronym in the sector. The acronym I learned that day was "CSEC." This term is used nearly every day. There are job titles and departments with CSEC in their title. I will break it down here.

C: The first C stands for "Commercially." We are all very familiar with that term and concept. A commercial enterprise has to do with goods and services. The phone service you are using today is a commercial enterprise. You pay your phone company each month, and they allow you to use their network and make calls. The restaurant you dine at is a commercial enterprise. You pay them money, and they provide you with food. Once you purchase your food, you can do anything you want with your meal. You can consume it, discard it, or share it. You own it and can do whatever you want with it. Concepts associated with "commercially" are "supply and demand," "profit and loss," "goods and services," "middleman," "product," and "supply line."

S: The S stands for "Sexually." We are all very familiar with this term. "Sexual" or "sexuality" is the basic and most intimate of human experiences. We learned in the sixth grade that's how other humans are made. More than that, human sexuality has to do with the most vulnerable, intimate, and personal part of our human existence. I think we would all agree that sexuality is best expressed in an environment of trust, commitment, honesty, and above all, consent. Sexuality defines us at our deepest core.

We know things are going in the wrong direction when we add the concept of "commercially" to the concept of "sexually." It doesn't make sense to combine those two terms. They don't fit together. It's not right.

E: The E stands for "Exploited." There are lots of nuances to this term, but the common understanding and definition of this is: "To utilize, especially for profit." "To use selfishly for one's own gain." Things are going from bad to worse with this acronym. Combining these definitions with the term "sexually" is wrong on so many levels.

C: The last C stands for... you guessed it, "Children." We are talking about Commercially, Sexually, Exploited, Children. You know... kids... Saturday morning cartoons, skinned knees and skateboards. Slumber parties and birthday parties. Play-Doh and field trips. Staying out until the street lights come on. Up too late and doing chores around the house. You know... children. That first sixth-grade crush on a cute boy or girl. That first awkward junior high school dance. Nervously thinking about what that first kiss will be like. Telling secrets to your friends and dreaming about the future. Birthday parties and Christmas mornings. Homework and book reports ... KIDS! That's CESC! It's the heartbreaking reality—or should I say nightmare—that some say as many as 300,000 children are living in the United States. And it needs to go away. There is no place in our society for this ridiculous reality. How in the world have we enabled and allowed "CSEC" to even exist? And what can be done about it?

Nelson Mandela once famously said:

"There can be no keener revelation of a society's soul than the way in which it treats its children."

If that's true, then we are hurting for sure. Something unimaginable is happening in our society. Children are being bought and sold on the streets and on the Internet. They are being treated like a product to be used and discarded. Children are being commercially, sexually, exploited, and this can't happen! We have to rise up and abolish this crime against humanity. For it to go on one more day is one day too long. For it to happen to one child, it is one child too many!

Appendix J
The Man in the Arena

"It is not the critic who counts; not the man who points out how the strong man stumbles, or where the doer of deeds could have done them better. The credit belongs to the man who is actually in the arena, whose face is marred by dust and sweat and blood; who strives valiantly; who errs, who comes short again and again, because there is no effort without error and shortcoming; but who does actually strive to do the deeds; who knows great enthusiasms, the great devotions; who spends himself in a worthy cause; who at the best knows in the end the triumph of high achievement, and who at the worst, if he fails, at least fails while daring greatly, so that his place shall never be with those cold and timid souls who neither know victory nor defeat."

— **Theodore Roosevelt**[22]

Contributors

John Richmond
Oree Freeman
Rachel Thomas
Rebecca Bender
Nola Brantley
Harmony Dust Grillo
Ryan Dalton
Sarah Godoy, MSW
Morgan Perry
Benji Nolot
Michelle Talley, LCSW
Captain Kent Wegener
Armand King

Authentic Masculinity Contributors

Ben Chambers
Adam LaRoche
Dr. Scott Lisea
Ryan Dalton
Kellan Lutz
Ray Bercini
Geoff LaTendresse
Louie Greek
Bazzel Baz

Acknowledgments

From Alan

I wish to extend my deepest gratitude to Jessica Midkiff, Oree Freeman, Rachel Thomas, Nola Brantley, Rebecca Bender, and Harmony Dust Grillo for contributing to this book. These women have survived decades of sexual exploitation and abuse through human trafficking, and this book would not exist without their generous contributions.

Jessica and Oree

A special shout-out to these two because you are my heroes. I am so much better for knowing you. Your input into this book, as well as my life, makes it real and authentic.

Special Agent Ryan Dalton and Captain Kent Wegener

I am grateful to the many professionals who generously contributed to this book. Their expertise added a measure of authority and credibility. And these two law enforcement professionals, in particular, added something special.

Sarah Godoy, MSW

Thank you for your ongoing input into the formation of this book. You spoke into this book extensively in the early stages through the lens of your human trafficking expertise and your academic background. Your input was invaluable.

Ben Chambers
You wonderfully spoke into this book through your male perspective combined with your writing background. Thank you for your ongoing encouragement and friendship.

Michelle Guymon and Adela Estrada
I am thankful for Michelle, who has been one of the pioneers of the anti-child trafficking efforts in Los Angeles. So many children are so much better off because of you. Adela, thank you for being an integral part of the anti-child-trafficking efforts in Los Angeles, and both of you gave important feedback into this book.

Authentic Masculinity Brothers
Thank you for being strong, healthy men who make the world a better place. Thank you for bringing healing rather than pain, and thank you for inspiring me and so many others.

Saving Innocence Advocates
You are my heroes. Thank you for your tireless pursuit of the kids we serve. You are strong, passionate, loving, pursuing, brave, smart, and funny. When all is said and done, having worked closely with all of you will be one of the highlights of my life!

John Richmond
What an incredible honor to have John Richmond write our foreword. His list of anti-human trafficking accomplishments is

long and distinguished, including his most recent post as US Ambassador to combat human trafficking. Receiving John's endorsement of this book and gaining his participation is a true honor.

Kim Biddle
And finally, I am incredibly grateful for Kim Biddle, the founder of Saving Innocence. Kim, you had the vision and courage to push against all obstacles as you stepped out in faith in order to pursue lost and hurting kids stuck in the horrors of sex trafficking. There are thousands of children who have new life because of your pioneering efforts back in 2010. Thank you also for taking a chance on me and adding me to your team.

From Jessica
David Bailey Sr. and Jr. (Papa and Uncle)
Thank you for your prayers and your constant advice. Thank you for always recognizing my strength and loving me uncon-ditionally. I love you both.

Supervisor Don Knabe
Thank you for your respect and friendship. Thank you for always protecting and honoring me. You are the meaning of a true friend.

Markeese Freeman
Thank you for always being my strong and caring friend. Thank you for teaching me so many valuable lessons I still use to this day. You've restored trust and faith in me, and I'm always thankful to call you friend and brother.

Chris Lim
Thank you for your patience and kindness and always taking time to teach and for always listening to me. Thank you for being a lifelong friend.

Alan Smyth
Thank you for being my friend, family, and mentor. You've sustained my faith in others and inspired a new light inside of me. Thank you for standing up and being the protector of me and my daughter.

Notes

1 A.M. Gray, *Warfighting: The US Marine Corps Book of Strategy* (New York, NY: Currency, 1994), 15.

2 *Braveheart*, directed by Mel Gibson, (1995; Burbank, CA: Paramount Pictures), DVD.

3 *Sex + Money: A National Search for Human Worth*, directed by Joel Angyal, (2011; Los Angeles, CA: Lot 3 Productions), DVD.

4 "Human Trafficking," Humantraffickinghotline.org, https://humantraffickinghotline.org/type-trafficking/human-trafficking#:~:text=Human%20trafficking%20is%20a%20form,services%20against%20his%2Fher%20will.

5 The Human Trafficking Institute, "2018 Annual Report" (Fairfax, VA), 3.

6 Jody Raphael and Brenda Myers-Powell, "From Victims to Victimizers: Interviews with 25 Ex-Pimps in Chicago," 2010 study by researchers at the DePaul University College of Law in Chicago (Chicago, IL), Sept 2010, 1. https://humantraffickinghotline.org/sites/default/files/From%20Victims%20to%20Victimizers%20-%20DePaul.pdf.

7 Alyssa Currier and Kyleigh Feehs, The Human Trafficking Institute, "2018 Federal Human Trafficking Report" (Fairfax, VA), iii.

8   Christina Villacorte, "Prostitution in Los Angeles: Some pimps control women with violence, others turn on the charm," *Los Angeles Daily News*, Updated August 28, 2017, https://www.dailynews.com/2014/05/18/prostitution-in-los-angeles-some-pimps-control-women-with-violence-others-turn-on-the-charm/.

9   The Human Trafficking Institute, "2018 Annual Report" (Fairfax, VA), 2.

10 Ellen Wulfhorst, "Without family, US children in foster care prey for human traffickers," appearing for the Thomas Reuters Foundation in *Reuters*, May 3, 2018, https://www.reuters.com/article/us-usa-trafficking-fostercare/without-family-u-s-children-in-foster-care-easy-prey-for-human-traffickers-idUSKBN1I40OM.

11 Sarah Godoy, Rebecca Sadwick, Kathleen Baca, "Shedding Light on Sex Trafficking," May 2016, https://innovation.luskin.ucla.edu/wp-content/uploads/2019/03/Shedding_Light_on_Sex_Trafficking.pdf.

12 US Department of Health and Human Services Office of Inspector General, "States' Prevention of Child Sex Trafficking in Foster Care," 2013. oig.hhs.gov. https://oig.hhs.gov/reports-and-publications/workplan/summary/wp-summary-0000396.asp#:~:text=In%202013%2C%20the%20Administration%20for,services%2C%20which%20include%20foster%20care.

13 Malika Saada Saar, "Stopping the Foster Care to Child Trafficking Pipeline," *Huffpost,* October 10, 2013, https://www.huffpost.com/entry/stopping-the-foster-care-_b_4170483.

14 Christian O'Neill, MSW, with input from staff at ECPAT-USA, "From Foster Care to Trafficking: An Analysis of Contributory

Factors," 2018, (Brooklyn, NY), 12. https://static1.square-space.com/static/594970e91b631b3571be12e2/t/5bb417f 5e5e5f0cff4dbd7ce/1538529305173/ecpat-usa-foster-care-report+%5Bwithout-bleed%2Bcropmarks%5D+Oct+2.pdf.

15 Lily Dayton, "How Neuroscience Can Help Us Treat Trafficked Youth," *Pacific Standard,* May 2, 2018, https://psmag.com/social-justice/how-neuroscience-can-help-us-treat-trafficked-youth%20.

16 Bender, Rebecca (@imrebeccabender), "Oregon native and sex trafficking survivor to speak at OSU," Instagram, December 6, 2020, https://www.instagram.com/p/Cld2bd NHVRm/.

17 Nicholas Kristof, "The Children of Pornhub," *The New York Times,* December 4, 2020, https://www.nytimes. com/2020/12/04/opinion/sunday/pornhub-rape-traffick-ing.html.

18 "How Porn Fuels Sex Trafficking," August 23, 2017, fight-thenewdrug.com, https://fightthenewdrug.org/how-porn-fuels-sex-trafficking/.

19 *Sex + Money: A National Search for Human Worth,* directed by Joel Angyal, (2011; Los Angeles, CA: Lot 3 Productions), DVD.

20 *A Few Good Men,* directed by Rob Reiner, (2001; Los Angeles, CA: Sony Pictures Home Entertainment), DVD.

21 "Report Trafficking," Shared Hope International, *https:// sharedhope.org/takeaction/report-trafficking/.*

22 Theodore Roosevelt, *The Works of Theodore Roosevelt, Vol X111*: "Citizenship in a Republic," Speech at the Sorbonne, Paris, April 23, 1910 (New York, NY: Charles Scribner's Sons, 1926), 506-529.

About the Authors

MEN! Fight For Me is co-authored by Alan Smyth and Jessica Midkiff, plus a host of other experts, both survivors as well as professionals in the field. The primary target of this book is the male audience. Alan is the primary voice speaking man to man, while Jessica provides expert testimony and insights throughout.

Alan Smyth

Currently, Alan serves as the executive director for Saving Innocence, an anti-human trafficking, community-based organization focused on the recovery and restoration of child victims of sex trafficking. Based in Los Angeles, Alan is responsible for direct services and business operations. You can learn more about Saving Innocence at www.savinginno-cence.org.

Alan is married to Sharon, and they have two children, Brittany and Trevor. Katy is their world-class daughter-in-law.

Jessica Midkiff

Jessica is a true "lived experience expert." She has survived ten years of commercial, sexual exploitation as well as having spent over ten years of advocacy work helping victims escape and recover. Jessica was instrumental in piloting many of the programs still used today which help trafficking survivors exit the life. In 2015, she was recognized as "Woman of the Year" in Los Angeles County for her extraordinary work in the field.

Currently, Jessica works for Saving Innocence and does a myriad of duties such as development support, administration, and helping interview prospective employees.

Jessica's greatest achievement is being Ja'Lynne's mom.

Made in the USA
Coppell, TX
23 July 2021